Official and Unofficial
US NAVY AIR PATCHES
1920s to Today

Derek Nelson and Dave Parsons

Motorbooks International
Publishers & Wholesalers ®

First published in 1990 by Motorbooks International
Publishers & Wholesalers, P O Box 2, 729 Prospect Avenue,
Osceola, WI 54020 USA

The information in this book is true and complete to the best
of our knowledge. All recommendations are made without
any guarantee on the part of the author or publisher, who
also disclaim any liability incurred in connection with the use
of this data or specific details

We recognize that some words, model names and
designations, for example, mentioned herein are the property
of the trademark holder. We use them for identification
purposes only. This is not an official publication

Motorbooks International books are also available at
discounts in bulk quantity for industrial or sales-promotional
use. For details write to Special Sales Manager at the
Publisher's address

Library of Congress Cataloging-in-Publication Data
Nelson, Derek.
    U.S. Navy air patches / Derek Nelson, Dave Parsons.
      p.   cm.
    ISBN 0-87938-447-6
    1. United States. Navy—Aviation—History.   2. United States.
Navy—Insignia—History—20th century.   I. Parsons, Dave.
II. Title.   III. Title: US Navy air patches.   IV. Title: United
States Navy air patches.
VG93.N44   1990
359.9′4′0973—dc20   90-5980
                                      CIP

On the front cover: This illustration of the VF–171 "Aces'"
patch was created by Valerie Nelson.

On the back cover: Three of the color plates from the book.

Printed and bound in Hong Kong

Contents

Foreword

The notion of doing a definitive guide to all Navy insignia—of tracking down who designed them, when and why, and then tracing the permutations of a design through the labyrinthine changes in squadron designations—is beyond the scope of this book. In fact, it is probably impossible. With some notable exceptions, no one knows when a given insignia was designed, and current members of squadrons rarely understand the roots of the insignia they wear. There are long-standing squabbles about the lineage of Navy squadrons, and there have been custody battles over popular insignia. The squabble over Felix is a case in point.

We have not tried, then, to create a comprehensive reference book. Our goal is to present a spectrum of insignia, some current, some defunct, some unofficial, some mysterious. We offer an anecdotal scrapbook, not a catalog or dictionary. We trace the history of insignia in general, with a glance at aircraft nicknames and fuselage markings. We examine squadron lineages, explain the origins of some current and obsolete Navy insignia, and track down the nominees for the "oldest" insignia. We review the Navy regulations governing designs, and describe how aviators have worn their patches from the 1940s to present. Along the way, we spend some time talking with historians and collectors.

Acknowledgments

We found very few written sources that could help us in our research for this book. That fact made the help of the following fine folks even more valuable. They lent us patches, told us yarns, provided guidance and gave us access to valuable material and information on both coasts.

Our deepest thanks to: Lt. Ward 'Nut Hair" Carroll, raconteur, editor and ace cartoonist; John Cataldo; Dennis Covello; Capt. Ken Craig; Lt. Cdr. Stephen "Rocky" DeVeer; John M. Elliott, Assistant Historian, Aviation History Branch, Naval Historical Center; Dr. John Garver, Cartographic Department, National Geographic Society; Roy Grossnick, Historian, Aviation History Branch, Naval Historical Center; Lt. Cdr. Andy Keith; Bob Lawson, editor of *The Hook* magazine, insignia collector and historian extraordinaire; Lyndon and Mary Kay Meredith, patch collectors who kindly let me visit and photograph at will; Peter Mersky, a source of aviation information both handy and extensive; the staff of *Naval Aviation News* magazine from World War II through the present; John Quarnstein, curator of the War Memorial Museum of Virginia in Newport News; Cdr. John "Pogo" Reid; Dave R. Smith of the Walt Disney Archives; Warner Stark, HQ Forces Command, US Army; and Carol Stevens, Managing Editor, *Print* magazine.

Chapter 1

Introduction

The military demands uniformity, and it usually gets it. The Navy lives in a world of haze-gray and khaki, where your rank is more important than your name, and every item of clothing is governed by regulations, diagrams and MILSPECs. Everything—hardware, equipment, furniture—is supposed to be utilitarian and depersonalized.

The situation is even more extreme when America isn't at war. Then the military does its best to promote an image of decorum and restraint. There's a huge difference between warriors and peacekeepers. The former are bellicose and abrasive; they're worried about incoming rockets, not grooming standards. In combat, commanders tend to give their men a lot of slack. When peace breaks out, it is no longer politically prudent to appear aggressive. The colorful excesses of combat—the grab-bag uniforms and the easier-to-get-forgiveness-than-permission creativity—vanish, replaced by barrages of paperwork and battalions of desk-jockeys.

There are chinks in this iron curtain of psychological stodginess, habits and traditions that run against the grain. The most vivid exception is the squadron insignia proudly worn by naval aviators. The patches on their leather flight jackets depict flying skeletons, flames and fangs, vultures, sharks, pirate flags and boxing gloves. These insignia are loud, violent and cocky, all the things to which the official, peacetime bureaucracy seems allergic. In the vast history of the military, has anything been as colorful, humorous and popular?

The images themselves don't owe their powerful popularity to excellence of drawing or design, or thematic cleverness; most were drawn by anonymous amateurs. The keys seem to be tradition and association, a draft of nostalgia and the intensely close-knit camaraderie of the people who wear the insignia on their flight jackets.

It's a shame that folks outside the Navy rarely get a chance to see the insignia. Part of the problem is the Navy's Tactical Paint Scheme (TPS), which specifies that

The back of Lt. Cdr. Andy Keith's flight jacket features a blend of official and unofficial designs, marking squadron tours (mostly with VA–34, 1976–79), cruises, achievements and deployments. His Kennedy cruises were between 1976 and 1979 (top center); VA–42 was his tour at the A–6 RAG (1975–76); a NATO cruise (bottom left, in 1976); and a Med cruise (bottom right, 1977). Keith entered the Navy in 1974, and is a career A–6 pilot.

Five patches from NAS Oceana-based fighter squadrons, representing enough history to fill several books.

airplanes must be painted in shades of gray, with squadron insignia (usually as a tail marking) in a single shade of gray about thirty inches square. With all the bright primary colors snuffed out, you may not even notice the insignia on Navy aircraft. And because the Navy periodically frowns on aviators wearing their flight jackets away from the hangar and the runway, you don't get much of a chance to even see the patches.

If you've ever scrutinized the jackets that people wear at air shows and veteran's reunions, or if you've just hung around with senior aviators for a while, you know that there are literally thousands of insignia. They come in freeform and geometric shapes, and in a spectrum of colors: There are the "Green Falcons" (VA–205), "Blue Diamonds" (VA–146), "Black Knights" (VF–154), the "Golden Dragons" (VA–192), and the VP–45 "Red Darts." The designs incorporate every conceivable weapon, slogan and creature (both real, imaginary and mythological). Some of these insignia belong to the hundreds of squadrons that have been redesignated or decommissioned through the years, often after going through a series of different insignia. Current squadrons, even those with old insignia, redesign them, or spin off variations.

The Navy currently recognizes a colorful hodgepodge of several hundred "approved" insignia, including a small handful of classic insignia from the 1930s and 1940s that survive under a grandfather clause, a sort of graphic fait accompli that makes the sailors and pilots happy and image-conscious admirals wince. In 1974, the Navy issued regulations for proposed new insignia. The powers-that-be grudgingly swallowed all existing insignia, but decreed that new ones must be dignified, and prohibited cartoons. The Air Force has written a similar set of rules.

Thanks to this wet-blanket approach, new Navy insignia look vaguely scholastic or corporate. That's been the trend since the early 1970s, and barring the sudden development of a sense of humor on the part of the Pentagon, it won't change. On the bright side, Felix the Cat and Old Moe have fought off the forces of blandness so far.

Pensacola's gosling

One of the best-documented insignia isn't a squadron insignia at all, per se, but it is one that all naval aviators see early on in their careers. It is the goofy gosling of NAS Pensacola, Florida.

John Elliott, now assistant historian at the Naval Aviation History and Archives department in Washington, D.C., started formal research on this emblem by

This insignia doesn't belong to a squadron and is rather silly looking, but it nevertheless is familiar to generations of Navy aviators—they run into it at Pensacola. NAVAIR Archives

writing a letter to *Naval Aviation News* in February 1974. Elliott then worked for the Smithsonian Institution, and mentioned a pamphlet he'd found that was issued by the Office of Public Relations at Pensacola, dated February 1944. That source called the insignia "J. Gosling," and credited it to Ltjg. Eddie Collins, who worked at the air station's Navigation Ground School. The pamphlet dated the insignia to Oct. 4, 1931, but Elliott thought it might be a bit older.

Four months later, the magazine printed a reply from R. A. Mortenson, who had known Collins before he retired. Mortenson wrote:

"In the days when NAS had seaplanes, the little duck, a bit awkward and humorous in his attempt to get up on his wings or land in the water, yet always endearing in his perseverance, made a fitting symbol of the student aviator. At that time, Naval Aviators were taught to stall out while six feet in the air; and then splash down, a landing not unlike the one J. Gosling is seen making."

Collins submitted two designs incorporating the duck or gosling. One was an American eagle nudging two of the little birds out of the nest. One, already out, was falling through the air with his eyes screwed shut and the other remained clinging to the nest for dear life. It was decided this was too complicated a design and J. Gosling was chosen. Assistant Secretary of the Navy Janke sent a letter congratulating Collins on his design.

At one time, a young man at the Naval Air Station was making up a booklet which included sketches of J. Gosling. He fancied he saw a resemblance between the NAS Duck and Walt Disney's Donald Duck, so he sent copies of his booklet to Walt Disney and asked permission to use the duck. Disney studios wrote back to say the duck could be used if the Disney trademark, WDP, for Walt Disney Productions, was printed beside it. And so the booklet was printed in just that manner, giving credit to WDP for a little duck that had hatched six years before their own Donald!

Chapter 2

Insignia roots

Tracing the roots of patch insignia offers plenty of room for colorful speculation and freewheeling guesswork. Although patch insignia might appear to be an aberration, it is important to recognize that military dress hasn't always been utilitarian and ergonomic.

Uniforms in the seventeenth, eighteenth and nineteenth centuries were downright gaudy, a far cry from the camouflaged combat gear in use today. Gold braid, hash marks, feather cockades, rainbow-colored ribbons and medals, badges, rank insignia, shoulder boards—all of these things found their way onto uniforms, particularly full-dress versions. And uniforms weren't always "uniform." During the American Revolution and the Civil War, officers often designed and tailored their own uniforms, following only general guidance.

Patch insignia, however, fall into a different category. They are intensely personal to a unit or squadron, and offer infinitely greater opportunity for humor and graphic expression. Instead of something bestowed by the establishment, such as a serivce ribbon or a medal, they tend to start at the bottom of the totem pole, dreamed up by the guys in the ready room and in the cockpit.

The standard explanation of patch insignia appeared in an article in the December 1952 issue of *Naval Aviation News*: "Not everybody knows it but the insignia idea dates back to the days when knights began wearing armor," the author wrote. "They couldn't tell friend or foe when all were encased in steel suits. So, a surcoat usually was worn with the heraldic emblems, commemorating some valorous incident or ferocious beast, like a dragon . . . Deeds and transactions were often sealed with their owner's armorial bearing."

Heraldry is all well and good, but it is full of hundreds of arcane rules and algebra-style, "lion-rampant-on-a-field-gules" terminology. But wolves riding torpedoes and Felix the Cat carrying a bomb don't belong in that arena. They are more modern, spontaneous and salty.

You need look back no further than the age of piracy. Take the case of Blackbeard, who was the definitive example of that breed. In *Blackbeard the Pirate, A Reappraisal of His Life and Times*, Robert E. Lee wrote that Blackbeard "became convinced . . . that courage and know-how were not sufficient if he was to become a successful pirate with the minimum of risk to his crew and ship. He needed an image. He was a student of psychological warfare far ahead of his time." Blackbeard braided his hair in little pigtails tied with colored ribbons.

Under the brim of his hat, he would tuck lit fuses made of hemp cord that burned slowly. Blackbeard didn't mind fighting, but he also knew that simply scaring his prey into submission without a battle was quicker and easier.

It is in this realm of "image" that one discovers a clear link with the roots of modern patch insignia. Consider Blackbeard's flag, which he flew on his ships, *Queen Anne's Revenge* and later *Adventure*. It showed a horned demon holding an hourglass in its right hand and a lance in its left hand. The lance pierces a red heart, which sheds three drops of blood. The hourglass symbolized "Your time has run out."

It didn't hurt that "sailors during the early eighteenth century were almost universally superstitious," Lee wrote. Blackbeard "proclaimed himself the Devil and played the Devil's role at every opportunity," Lee observed. As a result, "both victims and fellow pirates believed Blackbeard to be the Devil incarnate." It is tempting to make a direct connection to squadrons such as the Flying Tigers' "Hell's Angels," the "Sons of Satan" or "Satan, helmeted and goggled, superimposed on a ball of fire" (used by VB–5 in the late 1930s).

A ubiquitous combination—the saintly and the profane—appears in this insignia of VF–71, which was disestablished in March 1959. NAVAIR Archives

This World War I Army Air Corps insignia appears on a French light bomber flown by the American Expeditionary Force, circa 1918. NASM

At least in movies and on television, pirates flew the skull and crossbones. The author of another *Naval Aviation News* article, this one from the January 1950 issue, wrote: "One may say, 'What's in an insigne?' Well, many a fight has been won, and many a fair prize taken with no more show of force than a grimy skull and crossbones flying from the mainmast of a stout-rigged barkentine. Then there's the morale angle, many a young lad joined the forces of evil in order to stand beneath the grim but glamorous black and white flag of the privateer . . ."

One of the most comprehensive studies of military insignia appeared in the June 1943 issue of *National Geographic*, which claimed to show "the insignia of all the armed forces of the U.S." The more than 1,000 insignia pictured and described in that issue included Army shoulder sleeve insignia, and rank insignia, both of which are outside our current topic. However, a substantial subset—337, to be precise—were the "lively and apt insignia of military and naval aircraft." Speculating on the lineage of these devices, the author found them to be "kin to peacetime fancy jerseys on the gridiron, to pins of fraternal lodges and college fraternities." He also traced the use of such devices in America to George Washington, who devised badges during the Revolutionary War, and who used such things as colored cockades on hats and showy epaulets so that rank could be readily identified.

The devices, the article went on the explain, are "sources of pride in oneself and in one's organization. From this pride springs discipline . . . the essence of respect for self, for service, for country." Forty years later, in *The Smithsonian Book of Flight*, Walter Boyne agreed: "Squadron affiliations such as distinctive insignia cemented bonds between aviators."

The connection between fuselage markings and patch insignia is clear, although not necessarily simple.

Some fuselage markings became patch insignia and vice versa, others were one-of-a-kind paintings that were never put on patches or even shared by a squadron. Later, elements of patch insignia were adapted to tail markings.

During the war, fuselage markings and patch insignia were wildly popular. In "Aircraft Insignia, Spirit of Youth" (also in the June 1943 issue of *National Geographic*), Gerard Hubbard sketched the birth of such insignia at the hands of an anonymous squadron artist. "Hilarious, fanciful, or grim, his paintings are always young," Hubbard wrote. "After the artist has done his sketch and his squadron colleagues have given assent, down goes the paint brush into the can. Soon, on the side of another plane, a new symbol appears."

Pilots were decorating their aircraft well before World War II, of course. In his mammoth study, *The Official Monogram U.S. Navy and Marine Corps Color Guide*, author John Elliott (a retired Marine major) noted that as early as 1911, military aircraft were often customized because of "a personal desire for a particular marking which did not conform to a prescribed system."

"The early aviators applied many personal decorations to their aircraft," said Elliott's caption for a photo that shows a crude cartoon of Barney Google and his horse Spark Plug on a pre 1920 biplane, a Curtiss R–6.

A quick survey of other old photos reveals plenty of other examples from many countries. A Nieuport 17 from the Russian's 19th Squadron had a large, cheerful skull and crossbones that covered its tail when it was captured by the Austrians in 1917. The winter 1982 issue of *The Hook* shows a 1918 Curtiss N–9 that has an insignia painted on its fuselage. A much-published photo of the 11th Day Bombardment Squadron (which saw action in the offensives at Saint-Mihiel and Meuse-Argonne, France, in September and October 1918) shows the squadron members in front of their carefully lined up DH–4s. Each aircraft is decorated with the character Jiggs from the strip "Bringing Up Father"; Jiggs totes a bomb under his arm. Another photo in Elliott's book shows a black cat, superimposed on the numeral 13, painted on the fuselage of the only JN–4 approved to do aerobatics at the Marine Flying Field, Reid, Virginia, in 1920.

The black cat proved to have many lives as a fuselage decoration, by the way. Several photos of ex-military aviators who took up barnstorming after World War I include photos of aircraft decorated with this design. Skulls were another of the most popular of the early insignia and fuselage decorations. They were also the first device that the military bureaucracy tried to legislate out of existence (see chapter 8 on regulations).

According to Don Dwiggins in *The Barnstormers, Flying Daredevils of the Roaring Twenties*, "Barnstormers got publicity by posing pretty girls with their surplus ships," one of which was a Nieuport painted with the famous insignia of Charles Nungesser, who was France's third-ranking ace in World War I. Nungesser's insignia was a skull, with crossed bones beneath, surmounted by two candles and a coffin. One reference says that this pilot's first insignia appeared in 1915; it was a "crude skull and cross-bones" on a Voisin. The design was refined over time to the design described earlier and superimposed on a black heart, painted on his Spad SVII. The insignia was also painted on the aircraft used in his fatal transatlantic attempt of May 1927.

Many of the aircraft at Selfridge Field in Michigan in 1917 and 1918 sported fancy paint jobs—brightly striped tails, bands of colored stripes around the aft fuselage, personalized cartoons (a major named Boots had a cartoon showing a booted leg kicking the Kaiser in the rear). The 94th Pursuit Squadron used the war-bonneted Indian symbol it inherited from its predecessor, the Lafayette Escadrille, a squadron of American volunteer aviators who fought with the French before the United States entered World War I. An interesting detail of this insignia is the presence of the reversed swastika, a Sioux Indian symbol, on the bottom of the headdress.

Decorating aircraft continued with vigor during World War II, of course. Even the normally restrained British got into the act. In his unusual memoir, *The Last Enemy*, Richard Hillary recalled flying Spitfires for the RAF (Royal Air Force) very early in the war:

"Out before the huts crouched our Spitfires, seemingly eager to be gone, the boldly painted names on their noses standing out in the gathering dusk. Nearly every plane was called by name, names as divergent as *Boomerang*, *Valkyrie*, and *Angel Face*. Mine I called *Sredni Vashtar*, after the immortal short story of Saki.

"Srendi Vashtar was a ferret, worshipped and kept in the tool-shed by a little boy called Conradin: it finally made a meal of Conradin's most disagreeable guardian, Mrs. De Ropp. Conradin in his worship would chant this hymn: 'Sredni Vashtar went forth, His thoughts were red thoughts and his teeth were white, His enemies called for peace, but he brought them death, Sredni Vashtar the Beautiful.'

"I thought it appropriate."

The "Black Cat" squadrons during World War II tended to paint a basic feline symbol on their aircraft to represent their first mission. Many added nicknames, including "Black Mac," "Night Raider," "Alley Cat One Time," "We Get Ours By Night" and "Pugnacious Puss."

There is a fundamental link between aircraft nicknames, customized paint jobs, nicknames or call signs (in

Black cats were popular both as fuselage decorations and as elements in squadron insignia. This odd-looking Felix may be a relative of the one used for nearly half a century by VF-6 and its descendants, including *today's VF-31. The aircraft in this photo is both highly modified and clearly civilian, circa 1930.* NASM

a sample squadron, for example, you find Skull, Flinch, No-Show, Grits, Knockers, Soup, Weeds, Dog, Trog, Gatsby, Vapor, Cuddles, Otter, Repo, Gumby, Boo Boo) and squadron insignia. All fly in the face of military uniformity and depersonalization, and all are extremely popular with the guys in the trenches, workshops and cockpits.

The debate over the identity of the first Navy insignia will probably never be settled. Through the years, *Naval Aviation News* has led the investigation. Although it hasn't always been consistent, it has nevertheless turned up some intriguing possibilities. One nominee appears in the Jan. 15, 1945 issue, which carries a letter from the skipper of USS *Guadalcanal*. He included a photo of a coin-like object that says "Scouting Fleet One," with an eye between a pair of wings over the numeral. He wrote, "Enclosed you will find a photograph of the first squadron insignia . . . which was incorporated in a Christmas card in 1925."

Seven years later, the magazine introduced another possible device. "Available historic data on just what Navy or Marine squadron had the first insignia is a bit hazy," an article said. "Files of Naval Photographic Center, Anacostia, contain a 'squadron insignia' photographed in 1918 at Miami, Florida, then a Marine air training station. No data was available on what the crudely-drawn penguin or dodo bird stood for, nor to what outfit the emblem belonged." Furthermore, it doesn't say whether the bird appeared on a patch or a fuselage. Also, it looks like a pelican.

In 1950, the author of yet another article in that magazine wrote: "For argument's sake, the first naval aviation squadron badge of honor that can be recalled is the Hat-in-Ring emblem of VF–1. According to the oldest greybeard immediately available, this insigne was slapped on the first Navy airplane during the latter days of World War I."

Since that insignia is still in use by an Air Force squadron stationed at Langley AFB, Hampton, Virginia, and in the interest of trivia wagers, it is interesting to note a piece of information in Pierce Fredericks' *The Great Adventure*. He included an interesting footnote to the notion that the Hat-in-Ring was first in the fray in World War I. "The 95th Aero Squadron was the first actually up in the lines, but they were sent without any gunnery training or, indeed, even any guns on their Nieuports," Fredericks wrote. "Undaunted, they flew a patrol without guns," but were sent back for gunnery training. "In came the 94th, with its 'Hat in the Ring' insignia and Pershing's former chauffeur, now known as Lieutenant Eddie Rickenbacker."

SIRS:

Enclosed you will find the best photograph we could make of the first squadron insignia, an eye between a pair of wings, which was incorporated into a Christmas card in 1925. It was pretty hard to photograph and you may be able to do better in the Bureau of Aeronautics photo lab.
U.S.S. GUADALCANAL   COMMANDER, USN

In the Jan. 15, 1945 issue, Naval Aviation News *entered this contender in the long-running "first insignia" contest. The letter, from the commanding officer of USS* Guadalcanal, *said: "Enclosed you will find the best photograph we could make of the first squadron insignia, an eye between a pair of wings, which was incorporated into a Christmas card in 1925 . . . "* Naval Aviation News

From the earliest years, the human skull was the most popular single element of squadron insignia. Here it makes its appearance in the insignia of Marine Scout Bombing Squadron 244. Naval Aviation News

In 1952, *Naval Aviation News* further complicated the who-was-first question by announcing two *more* nominees for the honor. "One of the two real leaders appears to be the Ace of Spades squadron in the Marine Corps," an author wrote. "Its insignia, a black playing card, was designed by Lt. Hayne D. Boyden early in 1921. It won out over 350 other designs in a contest to choose a motif for the First Air Squadron, then in Dominican Republic." The squadron was the first Marine Squadron, and "flew the insigne all the way from Santo Domingo in 1921 to the Battle of Midway," the author pointed out. "As VMSB-231, the Ace of Spades squadron was one of the first two bombing squadrons on Guadalcanal."

In a recent book about the etymology of popular phrases, *Loose Cannons and Red Herrings*, author Robert Claiborne notes that the ace of spades "has long been intimately connected with battle, murder and sudden death." Keep in mind the fact that the word spade has nothing to do with shovels, but derives from the Spanish word for sword, *espada*. The book also makes another connection to pirates: "Handing someone the ace of spades was equivalent to giving him the 'black spot' described in *Treasure Island*: a message that he was due to be 'terminated with extreme prejudice.'"

The other 1952 nominee was good old Felix the Cat, which, *Naval Aviation News* noted, "appears to be the oldest Navy squadron insigne still in use." It pointed out that "another old one existed for a short time. Back in 1924 VOS–3 was serving aboard the cruiser Concord." Two lieutenants based an insignia on the label "from a jug of Bacardi rum."

In February 1953, yet another nominee for the oldest insignia turns up. A letter to *Naval Aviation News* describes an "early insigne used back in 1919 or 1920 in the old 'Atlantic Fleet Air Detachment.' This was before we had any designated squadrons, to my knowledge," the author wrote. "We had six old F–5–L flying boats attached to the USS Shawmut, an old minelayer that then was the flagship of the Atlantic Fleet Air Force . . . we decided we needed an insigne. We had a first class AP in the outfit

Playing cards in general—and the ace of spades in particular—were also an extremely popular device. In this one, first used by the VF–16A "Copperheads," the ace is combined with the aviator's wings. This insignia was used by VF–713 (which soon became VF–152, and much later VA–152) during the Korean War, with the addition of another drop of blood coming from the center of the card. The three drops were a tribute to three squadron pilots killed in air operations during the war. NAVAIR Archives

that drew this insigne, a grey Canadian goose in flight, on the skid fins of these old F–5–Ls."

And so the saga continues. One thing is certain, *Naval Aviation News* said: "By the end of World War II a squadron wasn't considered combat ready until every Ensign wore the outfit's coat-of-arms prominently stamped on his pajamas and largely displayed on the door and bumper of his BRC (big red convertible)."

Chapter 3

Squadron lineage

According to the Navy historians in charge of it, "The lineage and history of U.S. Naval Aviation squadrons has been a source of confusion since the birth of Naval Aviation in 1911. Much of this confusion arose from the terminology used by the Navy, the lack of a consistent policy in selecting the alphanumeric designations for squadrons, and the many establishments, redesignations and disestablishments of aviation squadrons."

The first system of nomenclature for aircraft, issued in July 1920, set the pattern: logic blended with inexplicable elements. For example, the system used the letter Z for lighter-than-air craft, and V for heavier-than-air. F, O, S, P, T and G were assigned for fighter, observation, scouting, patrol, torpedo and bombing for fleet aircraft of the V type. The first five letters were simply the first letter of the word. So why G for bombing?

Things certainly didn't get any better. According to NAVAIR's *United States Aviation, 1910–1980*, "There is no logical sequence for the numerical designation assigned the various squadrons . . ."

Designations were often recycled, which is why VF–1 from the World War II period has no direct relationship to VF–1 from the 1970s. Another complicating factor is the sheer number and types of squadrons. The reference just cited lists 248 squadron designations and abbreviations, from AAWS to ZX. In 1987, there were 282 current Navy aviation squadrons.

John Elliott, assistant historian in the Aviation History Branch at the Naval Historical Center in Washington, D.C., offers an example of how hard it is to trace the lineage of a current squadron, VA–75:

Date	Designation
7/20/43	VB–18, a bombing squadron
11/15/46	VA–7A
7/27/48	VA–74
2/15/50	Current designation

Others are more complex than that. Four different squadrons have been designated VF–41. Seven have been designated VF–1. According to Elliott, the lack of fixed squadron class designations and identification numbers "resulted in confusion of unit lineage almost to the point of utter disaster."

VF–11 has a particularly convoluted lineage. The original "Red Rippers" squadron was established in February 1927 as Fighting Squadron 5. It had these designations: VF–55, VF–5, VB–1B, VF–5B, VF–4, VF–41, VF–1A and VF–11. The latter squadron was disestablished in February 1959; on the next day, an existing squadron was redesignated VF–11, and promptly adopted the name and insignia of the original squadron. The official Navy historical archives credits the lineage of the existing "Red Rippers" only back to September 1950 (when the VF–11 that was its predecessor was established), and not back to 1927 and the previous VF–11.

Although squadron press releases and even printed histories use the term reestablished, that term is misleading. In the words of one aviation archivist, "A newly established squadron which uses the same designation of a unit that has previously existed may carry on the traditions of the old organization but it cannot claim the history of lineage of the previous unit." The current VA–36, for example, cannot trace its lineage back to VF–102, even though the first VF–102 was established in 1952 and redesignated VA–36 in July 1955, because that squadron was disestablished in August 1970.

Insignia are not a reliable indicator of the lineage or identity of a squadron. An article in the January-February 1987 issue of *Naval Aviation News* pointed out: "The lineage or history of a squadron cannot be traced using only its insignia because the same insignia may have been adopted and approved for official use by more than one squadron during different time frames."

As a result, the job of sorting out the provenance of a particular insignia—and trying to find out whether it was officially approved or not, who was using it and when—is a horrendous task.

One attack squadron insignia shows an advancing tiger, head on. It was used by VA–25. Notes in the official file show the kind of confusion that can result: the insignia was "apparently adopted between September '48 and July '59, with no record of official approval. However, it is reportedly used today (1970) by VA–65, which probably means it continued on as VA–25 was redesignated VA–65 on 1 July 1959. On the other hand, today's VA–25 used the 'clenched fist' insignia, which was originally VA–65's, approved by CNO June 1949. Apparently the squadrons exchanged designations 1 July '59 and also insignia!" the note concluded.

Given all these difficulties, it is no wonder that mystery patches appear, awaiting further research or the eye of a specialist in that area. The Torpedo Bomber Squadron 29 insignia (plate 8B) is an example.

A later note, on the VA–25 tiger insignia, said that VA–65 didn't get official approval to continue using the old VA–25 insignia when it was redesignated.

The original "Jolly Rogers" squadron was the VF–17 of World War II, established in January 1943 and disestablished in April 1959. The squadron commanding officer took over as skipper of VF–84, and got official approval to adopt the Jolly Rogers insignia in April 1960. However, there was no direct connection between the squadrons.

The current VFA–106, established in 1984, uses the same insignia as a previous squadron with a similar designation (VA–106), but its lineage doesn't include that squadron.

A similar phenomenon took place with the original VF–111 "Sundowners," which was disestablished in 1959. The next day VA–156 was redesignated VF–111, and adopted the Sundowner logo and nickname.

Another minor element that adds to the confusion about squadron names and numbers is nicknames, which typically come from vague and mysterious origins back beyond the memories of current squadron members. Two Navy squadrons—VF–32 and VA–145—use the nickname "Swordsmen," and a sword figures into the insignia of each. VF–32 started out as VBF–3 in February 1945. Their official (1962) insignia features a rampant lion on a shield, with wings above and a Latin motto. Another version has the lion holding a sword, and a third unofficial version (used during a couple of mid 1980s deployments) shows a cartoon "gypsy" Tomcat leaning on a sword, one in an endless series of insignia featuring Tomcat characters in various derivative poses.

The "other" Swordsmen are VA–145 of NAS Whidbey Island in Oak Harbor, Washington. In an earlier incarnation, they were the "Rustlers" (then based at NAS Dallas), with an insignia showing a charging longhorn bull loaded with bombs, mines and torpedoes. Their current, CNO-approved insignia is divided by a sword in the center, with lightning bolts on the left and a lion on the right.

The tangle of redesignations is what led to the rule against showing squadron designations as part of an insignia. The idea was to come up with a design that would be suitable even if the mission or designations changed.

The famous "High Hatters" (or "Tophatters"), now VF–14, are a case in point. The squadron started in 1919 as Air Detachment, Pacific Fleet. It then became VT–5, Patrol Squadron 4–1, Combat Squadron 4, VF–1 in 1922, and VF–1B in 1927, at which time the high-hat symbol was adopted. It was then redesignated VB–2B, VB–3, VB–4, VS–41, VB–41, VA–1A, VA–14 and finally VF–14 in December 1949. "Only such a general symbol as a high hat could have stood up as an insignia through all those changes—fighter, scout, bomber, patrol, torpedo," *Naval Aviation News* pointed out.

VF–102 was redesignated VA–36 in July 1955. On the same day, another VA–36 was both established and redesignated VF–102. Presumably, there is some obscure, bureaucratic logic to this sort of manipulation, involving squadron mission, aircraft and location. For the historian—even the professional, much less the amateur—it is nothing less than a nightmare.

Chapter 4

The 1930s and 1940s

When you dig into the history of Navy squadron insignia, you find plenty of bits and pieces of information; rarely do you discover any organized collections of data. Luckily, there are several exceptions to this rule.

One of these landmarks is the June 1943 issue of *National Geographic* magazine. Although the thousand-plus insignia included Army shoulder sleeve insignia and rank insignia (which are different kettles of fish), more than 300 were patch insignia. That issue, therefore, opens a window on the kinds of insignia then in use, and documents the existence of insignia that are still in use by the various military services. In terms of comprehensiveness and color depictions, the issue is without comparison as a reference for the early 1940s.

In the Navy squadron section, the illustrations include the "High Hatters" squadron's already well-known top hat, Felix with his bomb, and Old Moe (with blood on his scythe). Old Moe's squadron was then called VF–10; the article noted that the squadron's battle cry was "Mow 'em down!" VF–3's Felix didn't appear in a circle or with its yellow background, incidentally, but as a simple black figure against the fuselage, which was usually white. The yellow background appeared well after the war.

Another interesting document in the history of Navy insignia resides in the files of the Naval Institute in Annapolis, Maryland. It is a twenty-five-page, typewritten list of the origins of sixty squadron insignia. The list is dated January 1938, and is illustrated with crudely drawn versions of the insignia. The Institute's copy is stamped "Received June 20 1939 [by] Our Navy, Inc." of New York.

The text of this document was later reprinted, almost verbatim, in a series of "poster stamps" issued by the McLaurin-Jones Company of New York. Collectors could paste the stamps, which were about 1½ by 2 inches, into a small booklet that told the origin of each design in a small block of copy by each stamp.

Here's the text of the document's introduction:

"Naval aviation insignia may have a background of heraldry although a knowledge of this subject most certainly is not necessary in order to appreciate and understand the significance of the various symbols which have been adopted and reproduced on the fuselage of the planes of the various squadrons of the U.S. Navy.

"During the World War it became imperative that definite distinguishing marks be used on airplanes to prevent serious mistakes being made during periods of low visibility. This need brought forth the use of the Iron Cross insignia on the German planes and the tricolored circle on the aircraft of the allied forces. As the activities and strength in numbers of aircraft increased, the squadrons replaced the individual flyer. As pride in squadron organization grew and as victories were chalked up, the desire to be distinguished from other groups or squadrons asserted itself and the result was squadron insignia.

"This custom was retained by the military aviation services in the United States after the World War, but it was not until aviation 'went to sea with the fleet' that squadron insignia were adopted almost universally in the U.S. Navy. In most cases the squadrons have attempted to depict, by their insignia, the various functions or missions."

The text offers standard explanations of the origins and derivations of many early designs. They range from the simple to the convoluted, and from the clever to the bizarre. All in all, they present an excellent snapshot of the ideas behind early Navy insignia. What follows are excerpts from the text and descriptions of some of the designs.

VB–2: Pegasus appears in the design of Bombing Plane Squadron 2, which is ". . . a graphic adaptation of the Greek myth of Bellerophon and Pegasus. According to this old story, Bellerophon captured the winged stallion, Pegasus, and set out to slay the three-headed chimera. By diving three times over the monster, Bellerophon was able to strike off one of its heads on each attack. Since the primary mission of this squadron is dive-bombing, the insignia accurately symbolized the method of attack. The motto which appears over the figures is translated 'First to Attack.' It is written in correct Greek of the period in which the story originated." When fleet squadrons were reorganized in July 1937, Bellerophon's squadron had been designated VB–F2 aboard USS *Lexington,* which in turn had been VB–5B in 1935. A version of this insignia is currently used by VF–114 (see entry in Chapter 5).

VB–4: The insignia shows a diving black panther. Original colors are described as "Black and white panther; yellow claws; blue eye; teeth and the area around the eye, yellow; lips, red; inside of ear and end of nose, pinkish yellow." It is now in use by VA–35, but appears as black only.

VB–5: The text described the design as "the winged mesh of Satan, helmeted and goggled, superimposed on a ball of fire, represents the quick death and destruction which the planes of the dive bombing squadrons are capable of delivering . . ." See plate 7H.

VB–6: The insignia shows a wild goat, because these animals "inhabit the most precipitous and inaccessible

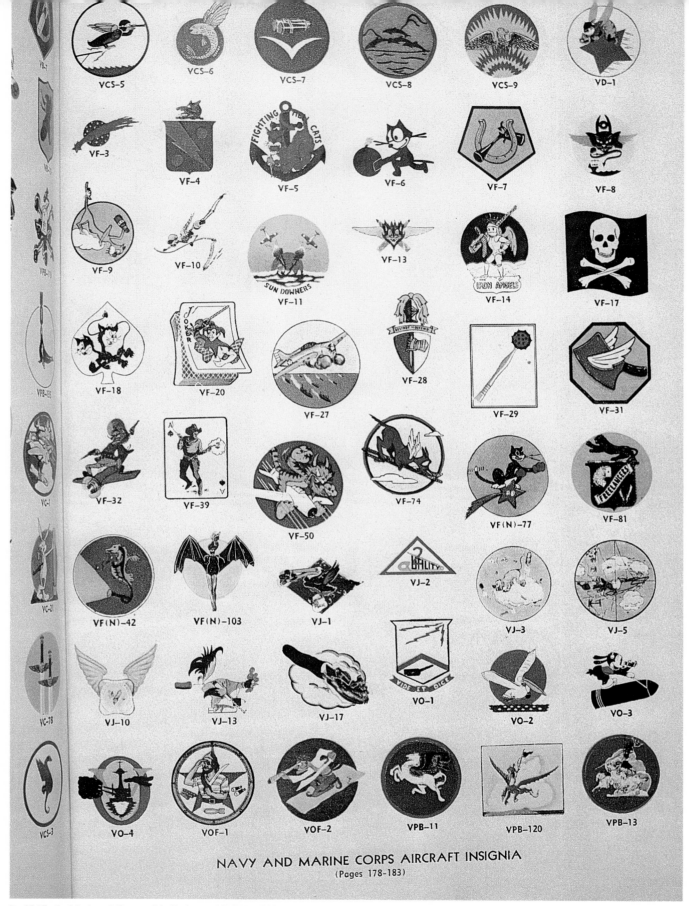

NAVY AND MARINE CORPS AIRCRAFT INSIGNIA
(Pages 178-183)

In 1945, the National Geographic Society published a 208 page book, Insignia and Decorations of the U.S. Armed Forces, a follow-up to their landmark June 1943 issue which included color plates of Navy squadron insignia. The magazine pictured 61 Navy squadron insig-nia, and the book added 89 more. Other color plates showed Marine Corps and Army Air Force insignia. Courtesy National Geographic Society

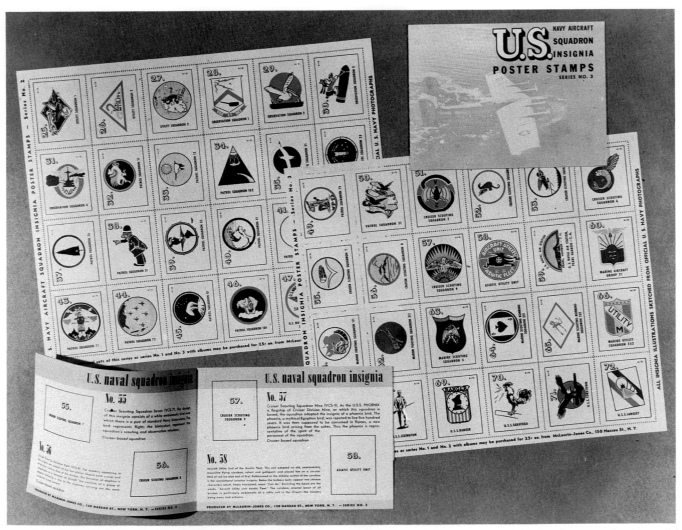

Examples of the "U.S. Navy Aircraft Squadron Insignia Poster Stamp" series, which collected the images and derivations of dozens of old insignia and made each set available for 25 cents on the commercial market. Naval Institute

heights of lofty mountains . . . They are remarkably swift, and display amazing agility and dexterity in leaping."

VS–41: This design ". . . dates back to the cruise to Honolulu in 1929, when information was received that the landplanes of the Squadron would be changed to amphibians . . . [they selected] a very busy-looking duck equipped with pontoons and wheels, wearing helmet and goggles. The usual explanation for the duck's pontoons is that the Squadron flies so far to sea that even a duck would hesitate to duplicate the trip without boats."

VT–6: This design was "the Great White Albatross, the largest seabird, capable of prolonged flight over open ocean, and often seen at a great distance from land. The wings of the albatross form a 'V,' the water spout forms a 'T,' and the fish in the beak of the albatross from a '6.'"

VP–2: This patrol squadron selected a cartoon figure of a rather rotund patrolman.

VP–3: According to the text, ". . . the elephant was originally pink, adopted simply because of the pleasing color. The pink, however, soon bleached to white and thus was

quite apropos of the old planes in use." In view of the popular connection between pink elephants and acute alcohol intoxication, the notion of a squadron using a pink elephant as a design seems ludicrous today.

VP–8: This squadron ". . . in 1933 discarded their old insignia of King Neptune sitting upon a rock in the sea and in its place substituted the 'Flying Eight Ball' . . . The significance is that the eight ball is the last to drop and it is dangerous to fool around anything with that dreaded number, including a squadron." It is interesting to discover that this squadron had a pre 1933 design, which would have been among the earliest of all insignia.

VP–10: The insignia shows a bomb over a compass with radio waves, the Big Dipper and Polaris. See plate 7A.

VP–12: This design is remarkable because it has one of the most elaborate explanations of all time: "Mt. Rainier, a prominent and welcome landmark for patrols returning over the fog from seaward, forms the background, while in the foreground is shown the Thunderbird surmounting a totem pole. The Thunderbird was regarded

16

by the Indians as a beneficient spirit. He was further believed to represent the war between light and darkness, and they believed that when the bird turned its head from side to side, as it does when angry, fire darted from its eyes (represented by lightning); that its wings were used for bows from which arrows or knives were shot. The lightning from the eyes (radio), the arrows and thunder from the wings (bombs, guns, etc.), and the legendary battles between the Thunderbird and the whale (submarines) all have a peculiar analogy to patrol plane operations."

VCS-2: Cruiser Scouting Squadron 2 "was organized in 1923. At that time certain characteristics of the planes assigned to the squadron were not conducive to good all-around vision, and the pilots described them as 'Blind as Bats.' "

VO-2: The design shows a pelican in flight above the sea, with binoculars around its neck. "The parallel between the pelican and the planes is undeniably close, to wit: his take-off is made in a shower of spray and a series of bounces . . . is keen on spotting his prey and seldom misses the catch . . . although he frequently wanders far from home, he makes a habit of returning." Insignia is currently in use (with minor changes) by VP–45. See plate 7B.

VO-3: Oswald the Rabbit riding "a major calibre shell."

NAS Pensacola: This explanation is among the most humorous. The design shows "a goose making a stall landing on the water . . . the goose is generally associated with a certain degree of foolishness and amusement. The silly countenance on this particular goose indicates lack of skill, while the excessive flapping of the undeveloped

wings proves a thorough willingness on the part of the student naval aviators to hard work. The smug expression indicates extreme pleasure at having arrived back on the surface of the water in a single piece. The large beak and mouth of the bird are typical of many of the students, for they make it possible for them to do their best flying while on the ground. The tremendous splash indicates the

VF-9

VP-31

VO-3

VF-42

VPB-129

An early version of the old VB-2 insignia. Other versions had the numeral 2 on the rider's shield. This basic design would go through many alterations, and would survive to be one of the oldest of all insignia still in use, most recently by VF-114. NAVAIR Archives

VP-2's patrolman survived long enough to be inherited by VP-31 (second from top), but is long gone now. The VP-31 and VO-3 insignia are discussed in the text about VP-2 and VO-3 in Chapter 4. These designs date back to the earliest days of Navy squadron insignia. All five squadrons are long gone. Naval Aviation News

skidding landing made by most students . . ."

VMB–2: This patch shows a running devil on a diamond-shaped field. In 1945, the squadron designation was VMTB–232.

VMS–2: The insignia shows an ace of spades on a circular field. "The Ace represents the high calibre of the squad-ron personnel, while the spade signifies the death-like precision with which the mission of the squadron is carried out."

VS–6: This one was "developed from a design of head-dress worn by the high priests of the Aztec Indian race during the rites of human sacrifice."

VS–2B: Dated 1930. The text says that it shows "the hunt-ing pointer dog. 'This seemed a fitting squadron insignia for a scouting squadron,' the squadron history report said, 'And definitely stopped the propaganda of certain Saratoga officers that the VS–2B insignia should be the monkey group, symbolic of see nothing, hear nothing, and say nothing.'"

The third major repository of knowledge about insignia is *Naval Aviation News*, mentioned earlier, which traces its own lineage back to a World War I bulletin. It was a Bureau of Aeronautics newsletter in the 1920s, and became a biweekly in 1935. It became a slick magazine in February 1943. Through the years, it published pictures of thousands of Navy insignia, many with brief squadron histories and updates. Insignia were a standard feature of the inside back covers through the 1950s and 1960s.

The magazine's photography during the World War II years was outstanding. Nevertheless, a careful study of those early issues, replete with plenty of photos of avia-

The pelican, here employed by VO–2B, would become a popular insignia device, and is still in use by some patrol squadrons. The huge sun is reminiscent of the well-known Sundowner insignia. NAVAIR Archives

VO–3's insignia was Oswald the Rabbit, a character created by Walt Disney in 1927. During negotiations with his film distributor in 1928, Disney lost the rights to the character. He bounced right back with Mickey Mouse, created that same year. Although color versions do not exist, the original specifications called for a red tongue, a dark pink shirt and dark blue pants; everything else is black or white. NAVAIR Archives

This wartime issue of Naval Aviation News *was marked "Restricted" just below the magazine nameplate. The dog at front right is wearing a Sundowner patch on his jacket. Naval Aviation News*

tors wearing leather jackets, doesn't reveal a single patch (much less a patch on a jacket) until April 1945; in that issue, one photo shows a pilot with a cloth flight suit that has an American flag at the top of the left sleeve.

Then it is another two years—until the September 1947 issue—that a patch-decorated G–1 (the Navy's

Patches of any type were rare when this carrier pilot, who had decorated his flight suit with an American flag, got his picture in Naval Aviation News *in April 1945. This very early Navy clothing decoration wasn't a squadron insignia and it wasn't on a flight jacket, but the trend was taking shape.* Naval Aviation News

Reservist pilots assemble at NAS Willow Grove, Pennsylvania, in 1947. Patches were just beginning to show up on G–1 flight jackets, such as that worn by the man at front left. Note that one man (standing at back, in the middle) wears a large skull insignia on what is either a flight suit or a cloth jacket. Naval Aviation News

For 40 years, Naval Aviation News *has been the finest (and often the only) source of information and pictures of squadron patch insignia. If you're near a library that has a collection of back issues, you're in luck.* Naval Aviation News

19

leather flight jacket) appears. That photo shows reservists in a classroom at NAS Willow Grove, Pennsylvania; a pilot in the front has a large patch on the right breast of his leather jacket. Curiously, another man in the back row seems to be wearing either a khaki flight suit or jacket, and has a very large skull in the same location.

Nevertheless, the old issues of the magazine are a gold mine of sketches, photos and trivia about insignia. For example, an item in the October 1944 issue reported that a squadron had adopted "the vociferous 'Hawky-Tawky' from the comic strip 'Barney Google and Snuffy Smith.'" The creature had "profuse and highly colored plumage," inhabited the South Pacific, spoke English, Japanese and twenty-seven tribal dialects. It was pictured in the insignia astride a Corsair, and had a Japanese flag painted on its beak.

Starting in May 1946, *Naval Aviation News* began running its long-standing series of back covers showing early squadron insignia. The skeleton theme was strong among the first batch: VT–43 had a winged, upright skeleton, VBF–17 had a cowboy skeleton riding a bomb, VF–82 had a simple skull over crossed guns and VMSB–244 sported a capped skull biting a bomb (surrounded by the name "Bombing Banshees"). VT–82 opted for a devil.

The June 1946 batch featured the now-familiar skull and crossbones of VF–17—it looked especially pirate-like because it was on a flag-shaped field. "Of special interest," the magazine noted, "is the VB–93 insignia which was derived from a humorous incident on a shakedown cruise when an aged pair of farm animals were killed during a strike at Culebra Island." The insignia showed the faces of a horse and cow, topped with halos.

Among the July 1946 entries was VF–20's tiny skeleton LSO (Landing Signal Officer) holding its paddles over a skull's eyes, with "Fighting 20" for teeth. VMF–514's insignia had a skull with a whistle in its teeth and several musical notes nearby; the explanation was that it represented the Japanese name for the F4U Corsair, "Whistling Death." VMF–115 used five cards, the ten through king of spades and a joker smoking a cigar—a figure that "personifies a plane with Major Joe Foss's ever-present stogie," the accompanying text said.

A shark, falcon, eagle, bat and crow all appeared in the August group; the only nonflying creature was a black sheep, which figured into VMF–214's insignia. The magazine explained why this squadron named themselves the "Black Sheep" squadron: "They felt they were the 'outcasts of the Marine Corps,' because when they were reorganized in 1943 they were not sent back into any major combat until the strikes on Rabaul."

The well-known symbol of the Wake Island "Avengers" appeared in September 1946, a V for victory mirrored in the island's shape. A boxing tiger, symbol of VMF–224, took a bow in October. The squadron was the second one into action at Guadalcanal "in the dark days of 1942," the caption read. "Led by Major Robert Galer with 13 Japs to this credit, the squadron ranks 9th in

This is the second set of insignia published by Naval Aviation News, *in June 1946. With the outstanding exception of VF-17's Jolly Roger (note the flag-shaped field), most are long gone and not particularly memorable. The trend toward a sort of Noah's ark of animals, however, was already distinguishable.* Naval Aviation News

This set of early insignia, from the November 1946 issue of Naval Aviation News, *features a design by Milt Caniff at upper left.* Naval Aviation News

Marine Corps aviation in kills with 119 planes." Soon VMF–322 adopted a vulture that also wore boxing gloves.

A Milton Caniff drawing appeared in November's batch, an intricate drawing of a hooded figure holding a sword, constellations of stars and three armored, winged horses carrying armored riders (symbolizing night fighters, night torpedo and night bomber aircraft). The insignia was used by Night Carrier Air Group (CVG–52). Also that month, VT–5's feline biting a bomb recalled VMSB–244's insignia. Wolves were selected by VBF–3 and VC–69.

In January 1947, the insignia of Carrier Air Group 81 was a montage of its three squadrons; the lower left quadrant was occupied by a flying, winged razor, holding a gun in its mouth and dropping bombs. This insignia was used by the modern "Hell Razors" squadron, VA–174, until they were disestablished.

A plain, green pawn on a white shield appeared in February as the insignia of VF–4B; today it is used by VA–42, the A–6 FRS (Fleet Replacement Squadron). VMF–122's was more complex: a wolf riding in a poison bottle that had the Corsair's gull wings and tail assembly. It is curious to note that the wolf is holding up the middle finger of its right hand.

A distinctive Disney drawing showed up in March 1947: a peg-legged Black Pete figure, with a machine gun instead of a wooden leg, holding sword aloft. Used by VF–14–A, the insignia honors a captain named Hoskins,

skipper of USS *Princeton* (CV–47), who lost a leg in battle. Of interest is the famous Disney signature printed at the bottom of the design.

Several symbols still in use appear in Air Group 1's insignia in April: the top hat, a round, black bomb, a rampant lion and the Red Ripper's shield.

And so it goes through the years—a fantastic Noah's ark of creatures (both natural and imaginary), with a pink elephant, bears, panthers, storks, dogs, grasshoppers, a St. Bernard, an octopus, Indians, dragons, a griffin and turtles. The parade ranges into mythology (Odin, Pegasus), images of violence (bombs, guns and torpedoes), gambling (flying eight-ball, ace of spades), Satan with a persistent undercurrent of skulls (of the first twenty-seven insignia shown, eight had skulls or skeletons) and cartoons (Oswald the Rabbit).

The pictures offer excellent insight into the roots of modern insignia, as well as a gold mine of trivia. The dragon from the old VT–3 insignia crops up as an element in the current insignia for VA–192 and VAQ–130, for example. There was a ram on the old VB–6 insignia, and there is a ram's head on the current VA–83 emblem. The old VP–9 insignia (a silhouette of a flying goose, facing left, below a sun) looks a bit like the modern VP–22 design. The sea horse in the old VCS–3 design appears in the current insignia of both VA–55 and HS–1. And the ace of spades that was the focal point of the old VMS–2 insignia now appears in the modern device of VF–41.

Disney

Although most insignia were sketched by novices, that wasn't always the case. The outstanding exceptions are the hundreds of insignia produced by the Walt Disney studios during World War II.

The saga began in the summer of 1941. Lt. E. S. Caldwell, then at the Naval Operations office in Washington, D.C., wrote a letter to Walt Disney asking for an emblem for the torpedo boats of the so-called mosquito fleet. According to a *Life* magazine article on May 26, 1941, Disney studios responded with "a little mosquito, streaking through the water with a tar's hat on his head and a shiny torpedo held between his many legs." The Disney design "made such a hit that every torpedo boat in the fleet soon had a Disney mosquito," the article said. Soon, the studios "were bombarded with requests . . . By last week it was clear that Disney and his artists had created a whole new system of heraldry, comparable to the ancient knightly arms."

At the time the article appeared in *Life,* the studio had completed more than 200 designs, and expected to do at least 500 more. Two artists were working full time on the job—(the article mentions gagman and story director Roy Williams and draftsman Hank Porter.)

The article illustrations included designs drawn for observation squadrons (a bug with binoculars on a cloud, and an eagle with a telescope), pursuit squadrons (a falcon with helmet, goggles and boxing gloves; a pelican with a machine-gun-toting bug in his bill; a head-on view

of a bulldog with lightning bolts on his boxing gloves and stars on his shoes).

According to Disney archivist Dave Smith, most of the insignia were for military units that were disbanded after the war. A December 1952 article in *Naval Aviation News* said: "During the war, the Walt Disney studios drew many dozens at the request of the Navy squadrons who had no artists. These featured ducks, mice, dogs and other caricatured animals. As squadron missions changed since the war or the units got new types of planes, these insignia gradually have been replaced."

Smith said although it seems certain that some Disney insignia are still in use somewhere in the sprawling military aviation establishment, it is hard to track them down. The Disney archives in Burbank, California, keeps copies of all such insignia, but it files them by the squadron designation at the time Disney artists drew the insignia. Those designations are certainly no longer current, and may be different than the squadron's original designation.

Smith did point out that he'd recently gotten a call from a Marine Corps fighter squadron that wants to bring back its old Disney insignia of a bulldog with boxing gloves. Given the official prohibition against showing cartoons and animals doing human things, the rebirth of any Disney classics seems unlikely.

Another footnote to Disney's massive contributions was a contest that the Walt Disney studios conducted for the BUAER *News Letter* (predecessor of *Naval Aviation News* magazine) in 1943. A Navy lieutenant was working

This complex design is easily recognized as a Disney contribution, this one for VF–35 (part of CAG-35). The gloves and feet were red, and the handle of the scythe was bright blue with a yellow streak in the center. NAVAIR Archives

This familiar Disney character, Black Pete, long survived the squadron it went to war with—VF–132—which was aboard USS *Princeton (CV-37) in December 1948 when this design was submitted for approval. Pete was a recurrent foil to Mickey Mouse, and was copyrighted by Disney back in November 1928. See also plate 10A.* NAVAIR Archives

on training literature at the studio, and came up with the idea of holding a cartoon contest among the Disney artists, specifically for the *News Letter*. The contest produced a "2–foot pile of freshly drawn samples" for the publication.

The Disney studios were careful to maintain a copyright on the designs, and the Naval Air archives contain many copies of the licensing agreements. A typical one is dated Nov. 5, 1943, signed by the vice president of Walt Disney Productions at Burbank, California. In it, for the sum of one dollar, Disney granted "unto the United States Government, as represented by the Secretary of the Navy . . . the exclusive and perpetual right and license to reproduce and use the following motif, device or design . . ."

The description of the insignia for VF–132 (plate 10A), according to the agreement, dated January 1946, follows:

"Caricature of Pete wearing pirate's costume carrying model destroyer under left arm and holding saber in upraised right arm. His peg leg is caricatured as a machine gun which is emitting fire from barrel. A circle forms the background."

Since the character of Pete had already been copyrighted by Disney, the licensing agreement contained a clause that stipulated, "The licensor retains and reserves to itself all rights in and to the aforesaid character, including all copyrights thereto, subject, however, to the Government's exclusive right to use and reproduce the 'design' hereinabove described."

Although most people know about Disney's wartime contributions, they may not know that the studios continued to draw insignia for military squadrons even after the heyday of World War II, well into the 1950s and 1960s, Dave Smith said. In 1959, for example, they drew an airborne camera, wing and anchor for Light Photographic Squadron 61 at Miramar Naval Air Station, San Diego. They also drew insignia for Air Force and Army aviation units up through the Vietnam era. According to Smith, the grand total to date is 1,200 insignia.

In the late 1970s, a Disney character called Lambert, the Sheepish Lion decorated the tails of VP–90's Orions at NAS Glenview, Illinois.

Chapter 5

Fighter squadrons

Fighter squadrons were one of the handful of original types of squadrons in the Navy. Given their long history, and compared to the wild perturbations in the nomenclature of other types of squadrons, it is remarkable that their title has stayed clean and simple. As a rule, their insignia have been the most colorful and gutsiest of all.

The squadrons listed here are only a fraction of all of the Navy fighter squadrons that have existed. Some squadrons were included because of their fame and their illustrious history. Others appear because they have interesting or curious insignia. In still other cases, squadrons appear because their insignia fill in gaps in the thorny, convoluted history of Navy aviation, or because their insignia pose interesting puzzles.

Tracking down the lineage of a given squadron can be extremely difficult. Four different, unrelated squadrons have had the designation VF–4, for example. *Seven* squadrons have been designated VF–1. Welding that pattern to the shifting cast of insignia—which change, go away, come back, or cohabit—is mind-boggling, indeed. There is no simple, cross-referenced, accessible reference list, either. In all cases, at least one reliable source and preferably a primary source (contemporary to the design) is the source of the information about a squadron's insignia and lineage.

Two variations of the basic VF squadron—VBF and VF(N)—are also included in this chapter. VBF meant "Bomber-Fighter squadron"; these squadrons were

The long-lived VF–5 design dressed up the skipper's Grumman F2F–1 in August 1938. In the pre-Tactical Paint Scheme days, aircraft were vivid; this one featured red on its engine cowl, fuselage band and upper-wing chevron, and green on the tail assembly (designating that the squadron was assigned to USS Ranger*). NAVAIR Archives*

established in early 1945. The three existing VF squadrons that have a VBF designation in their lineage were redesignated from VBF to VF in November '46. VF(N) meant Night Fighting Squadron, a short-lived designation.

VF-3A

When this squadron flew off the USS *Roosevelt*, it incorporated a caricature of the jaunty FDR (plate 10M), with top hat and cigarette holder, above a silhouette of the carrier and with the signal flags spelling the squadron's initials along the left side. It was pictured in the July 1948 issue of *Naval Aviation News* as VF-3-B.

VF-4A

This squadron became the modern VF-32 "Swordsmen" in August '48, and its insignia (plate 10I) is still in use.

VF-5

The insignia is a yellow, five-pointed star behind a descending eagle, and appeared as early as 1938. Its old nickname was "The Striking Eagles." This insignia is now in use by VF-51 (plate 5B). The insignia used by HS-2 in the mid 1960s featured an almost identical eagle.

VF-7

In the *National Geographic* book, VF-7's insignia (plate 10F) appears along with VB-7 (a bomb), VT-7 (a torpedo) and CAG-7 (plain), all using the same basic horseshoe design.

VF-11 "Red Rippers"

The original "Red Rippers" squadron was established in February 1927 as Fighting Squadron 5, the second fighter squadron created in the Navy but the first one that remained a fighter squadron since its inception. Its lineage includes squadrons designated VF-5S in 1927, VF-5B in 1928, VB-1B in 1928, VF-5B in 1930, VF-4 in 1937 (on the USS *Ranger*), VF-41 in 1941, VF-4 in 1943, VF-1A in 1946 and VF-11 in 1948. The original squadron was disestablished Feb. 15, 1959; thereafter, VF-43 was redesignated VF-11, and inherited the emblem. Together, the two VF-11s have flown twenty-one different aircraft types, operated from seventeen carriers and have been redesignated eight times. At least thirty-five admirals have worn the insignia. As of this writing, VF-11 flies F-14 Tomcats and is based at NAS Oceana, Virginia.

In an extensive study of the history of the "Rippers," Jeff Ethell wrote, "Mystery surrounds the origin of the name 'Red Rippers' . . . At the Air Races in Chicago, the press insisted on calling VF-5B the 'High Hats' (VF-1B at the time), and the Fighting Five pilots were highly insulted. When the reporter asked what the squadron was called, the pilots translated the unprintable insignia: the 'horny' boar's head, the 'bunch' of bologna below it, the 'two-balled' emplacement of the heraldic shield which, with its slash, indicated the owners to be illegitimate. The reporters decided that they couldn't say anything about the insignia, and apparently made up a colorful nickname, because the next day the phrase 'Red Rippers' showed up in the newspaper articles."

VF-6's shooting star was among the oldest designs, now—like so many other old designs—long gone. NAVAIR Archives

A Ripper by any other designation—in this case, VF-5B, Aug. 1, 1930. If these aviators look young, they are. The photo includes one ensign, 13 lieutenants junior grade, three lieutenants and the senior officer present—a lieutenant commander (fifth from left, front row). Note the patchless jackets, mascot at center and the missing "baloney" beneath the boar's head. NAVAIR Archives

The Red Ripper insignia decorates the fuselage on this F3B-1 Seahawk. VB-1B was the second designation of the original "Red Ripper" squadron, circa 1920 to 1930. NAVAIR Archives

Air Group One

As depicted in the April 1947 issue of Naval Aviation News, *"Air Group One's rampant lion represented torpedo bombers, the smoldering bomb the fighter-bombers, and the buckler the Red Ripper squadron." Insignia aficionados will be reminded of the Tophatters and of Felix's bomb.* Naval Aviation News

The squadron history includes a 1933 document entitled "Significance of the Squadron Insignia." It says, in part:

"The wild boar is the ugliest snouted, worst-tempered, fastest-moving creature in the whole Noah's Ark of nature, and is as full of tricks as a 13-spade bridge hand . . . He is the only animal that dares drink at the same pool with the tiger . . . he is as shifty as a pickerel in eel-grass . . . The Boar's Head is taken directly from the one that graces the label on the Gordon's Gin bottle. The scroll effect under the head is a string of sausage—the good line of bologna which all members of the squadron were to be adept at 'shooting.'" The balls on the shield might be called balls of fire; actually they were supposed to typify good, strong masculinity. The bolt of lightning is the bar sinister—sign of bastardry. The whole theme was worked into sort of a toast or creed with which the squadron members were to begin and end all good drinking bouts: 'Here's to us, the Red Rippers . . . a damn bunch of gin drinking, bologna slinging, two-balled, he-man bastards.'"

The first appearance of this famous emblem (plate 5A) in *Naval Aviation News* was in January 1951, when the squadron was then known as VF–11. In that rendition, beneath the boar's head, was an actual string of sausages (four to be exact). This feature later turned into a sort of decorative scroll, and the magazine caption refers to it as "sausage."

A 1938 description of the derivation of the insignia is that the "crest is the head of a wild boar which depicts that characteristics of the pilots when operating against the enemy. The bolt of red lightning suggested the squad-

A rare 1951 version of the Ripper logo with sausage instead of braid beneath the boar's head. Although the explanation of the insignia always refers to the braid as sausage or baloney, it doesn't look like it in most depictions. Naval Aviation News

Compare the braid beneath this boar's head with the sausage version. The fangs on this boar are also longer. NAVAIR Archives

One of the most striking nametags in naval aviation features the "Red Rippers" squadron's boar's head, an element of their official insignia.

Lt. Cdr. Joe Horvath was with the squadron from 1986 to 1988, a late tour in his career, which started when he flew F-4s in 1973.

ron's nickname of 'Red Rippers,' a sobriquet that has followed it since the adoption of the insignia."

In December 1952, *Naval Aviation News* cited the "Rippers" as "Running neck and neck for second place [of the oldest insignia still in use] are two of the most famous Navy squadrons—VF–11's Red Rippers . . . and VF–14's High Hatters . . . Both emblems date back to 1927 . . . The Red Rippers started out as VF–5B on 3 January 1927. Their highly-colorful insigne was modified several times. Today it features a boar's head—reputedly from the Gordon's Dry gin label, over a length of braid (some claim it is a string of bologna)."

VF–14 "Tophatters"

It is ironic that one of the simplest of all squadron insignia—a formal, black top hat in a plain circle—would survive to be among the oldest ones still in use. But that is the case with the insignia of the VF–14 "Tophatters" (plate 5A).

This squadron indirectly traces its roots back to September 1919. Since that time, according to the squadron history, the two "Tophatter" squadrons have flown twenty-two different aircraft, had a total of fourteen designations, operated from seventeen different aircraft carriers and several battleships.

The squadron's first skipper was Capt. H. C. Mustin, one of the earliest naval aviators, back when the squadron was called Fighter Plane Squadron 1. The squadron flew observation missions, and later scouting, attack and fighter missions. It began its carrier flights on USS *Langley*, the Navy's first aircraft carrier, in 1926. The next year it set an early record for traps (arrested landings) in one day: 127.

During World War II, squadron pilots saw action during the invasion of North Africa, in air strikes in Norway and during the assault of Iwo Jima.

Here's the 1938 explanation of the origins of the insignia, then in use by VB–3:

"The 'High Hat' insignia was adopted in June 1927. Prior to that time the insignia was a diving eagle which lost favor because of its resemblance to a parrot used to advertise a well-known brand of chocolate [Ghirardelli

A couple Red Rippers designs adorn this aviator's flight suit in the form of a patch (on his right) and nametag. This photo was snapped at NAS Oceana, Virginia, in October 1982.

chocolate in a can]. While casting about for an appropriate insignia an idea was furnished when one of the pilots of the squadron appeared in a very battered top hat. The 'High Hat' became forthwith the insignia of the squadron, at that time designated 'Fighting One.' As someone in the squadron at that time aptly remarked, 'There was no special reason—it just seemed like a good idea at the time.'"

This tale was repeated in a 1943 article in *National Geographic*, which listed the derivations of various designs. The squadron's first nickname, incidentally, appears in historical records as either the "High Hats" or the "Highhatters."

A letter in the May 1975 issue of *Naval Aviation News* attributes the idea to Gerald Bogan, skipper of Fighting Squadron 1 in 1926 and later a vice admiral. Bogan said the Rickenbacker's 94th Aero Squadron design (the Hat in the Ring) was his inspiration.

In the NAVAIR archives is an issue of "Plane Talk of USS Saratoga," dated "At sea, January, 1928." One article mentions VF–1B, Fighting Squadron 1, "composed of F2B airplanes, whose purpose is to combat enemy planes in the air. The VF–1B squadron's insignia is a High Hat., the wherefore of the High Hat being that the Pilots are good and know it. And how!"

A recent squadron public affairs officer has seen photos dating back as far as 1929 showing the insignia on squadron aircraft. In July 1937 the High Hat was in use by VB–3 on the USS *Saratoga*. Today, the squadron has the insignia painted on the walls and passageways of its squadron buildings and tiled onto the floor of its ready room aboard USS *Kennedy*, the aircraft carrier on which it deploys. Squadron members wear it on their helmets as well.

Perhaps it is the stark simplicity of the design that has helped make it so attractive to filmmakers. Sharp-eyed fans of old films will notice the familiar insignia in *Hell Divers* (MGM, 1931). The film stars Wallace Beery and Conrad Nagel as feuding members of a Navy squadron called VF–1B, flying F8C–2 Helldivers aboard USS *Saratoga*. Beery was in fact commissioned as a Navy lieutenant commander and got his real-life wings in 1934. The top-hat insignia also appears in the 1949 Warner Brothers film *Task Force*, a semi-documentary about the history of

The classic Tophatter insignia decorates F2B-1s. USN

Corsair to Corsair II

This illustration appeared in the July 1971 issue of Naval Aviation News. *This older version of the Tophatter insignia is making a comeback among new members of the squadron. Note that Captain*

In 1950, Ens. J. B. Morin was photographed in his F4U Corsair aboard USS Wright (CVL-49) during a Mediterranean deployment. Nearly 6,000 hours and 900 carrier landings later, Captain J. B. Morin, as Commander, Light Attack Wing One, was flying an A-7E Corsair II at NAS Cecil Field, Florida. This month, Capt. Morin becomes Commanding Officer of LPD-3.

CAPT JIM MORIN

Morin's G-1 jacket has accumulated a few more patches in the intervening years. Naval Aviation News

This version of the Tophatter insignia is the most current and common of the classic design, although some depictions lack the shading on the banners. Naval Aviation News

Naval aviation (from 1921–48) that stars Gary Cooper. A still photo taken during the filming (aboard USS *Antietam* in late 1948) shows a Boeing 100 modified as an F8C–2 Helldiver in one of the historical sequences; it is taking off from a carrier and bears the top-hat insignia on its side.

Old versions of the squadron patch simply featured a large top hat, with no slogans. This version has recently been adopted by younger squadron members. By the mid 1960s, the logo had "Fighting 14" on the top banner, and the word "Tophatters" on the bottom banner.

The squadron held a 70th anniversary celebration at NAS Oceana, Virginia Beach, in September 1989, and laid plans for an even grander blowout for their 75th. At the 1989 splurge, squadron veterans met and exchanged tales about when the Helldiver was state of the art, and mighty fast—it would go 270 mph, one former squadron member told a Norfolk journalist, "with the nose straight down and full throttle."

VF-14A "Pegleg Petes"

The Pegleg Pete design has been used by at least three Navy squadrons. In the March 1947 issue of *Naval Aviation News*, it appears with the designation VF-14-A, and has the Disney signature beneath it. A photo in the NAVAIR archives, shows a squadron designated VF-132 aboard USS *Princeton* (CV-37) using the design; the photo is dated Nov. 22, 1948. *The Hook*, Spring 1984 shows a VBF-81 "Pegleg Petes" patch (plate 10A).

VF-15

Milton Caniff, author of *Terry and the Pirates,* designed the insignia for Fighting Fifteen—a flaming cat with Navy wings. The squadron was established Sept. 1, 1943. The insignia shows a demonic face in the center of a pair of wings, tilted to the right, with flames coming from behind. Its first skipper, Lt. Cdr. David McCampbell, had thirty-four kills, won the Navy Cross twice and the Medal of Honor. He was the leading Navy ace in World War II. Flying off USS *Essex,* the squadron destroyed 313 aircraft in the air, an equal number on the ground or in the water, and damaged or sunk more than 500,000 tons of enemy shipping. See plate 10I.

VF-16-A

This emblem shows an arrowhead piercing a winged ace of spades card (plate 5A), with two drops of blood dripping from the ace. It appeared in *Naval Aviation News,* August 1948. Squadron has been disestablished.

VF-19 "Satan's Kittens"

This squadron was established Aug. 15, 1943, at NAAS Los Alamitos, California, by Fighting Squadron 19, flying F6F Hellcats. "Considering the tomcat a natural and savage fighter worth emulating, VF-19 chose this rugged symbol of strength for its insignia. Arraying the cat in Satan's robes, the squadron drew this savage figure riding out of the clouds hurling thunderbolts in fury. The cat's fangs and claws were bared, ready for attack with no holds barred. The squadron's nickname came naturally— 'Satan's Kittens,'" according to the squadron history. It is standing on a pitchfork that is stuck in the cloud, and its tail is looped around the handle. In 1959, the insignia was described as a "fiendish cat hurling pitchfork and light-

From biplanes to Tomcats, the classic top hat has ridden on them all.

ning bolt." It is facing right, with the cloud at lower right. See entry for VF–191 and plate 10H.

VF–21 "Mach Knockers" and "Freelancers"

In the September 1951 issue of *Naval Aviation News*, this squadron's insignia was an upright, mailed fist, shattering the words MACH against a red-and-black striped background. A photo caption says the fist is "smashing the mach meter needle, typifying the squadron nickname, 'The Mach Knockers.'" This squadron became VA–43 and then VF–43 (plate 5B), eventually deleted the word MACH and adopted the nickname "Challengers." They flew the TA–4 as the instrument RAG (Replacement Air Group), eventually flew A–4s, TA–4Js, F–5s and now F–16s. VF–43 changed the fist to represent their new role as an adversary squadron.

The VF–21 "Freelancers" (plate 5A) is a different, unrelated squadron, now based at NAS Miramar. This squadron's emblem, dating back to 1952, was "a panther denoting hard striking power, lightning in the 'V for victory' shape and a 'grand slam' of cards, for 'all enemy aircraft shot down.' Freelancers is from the fighter director term freeing them from CAP duty to pursue the enemy." In the August 1961 issue of *Naval Aviation News*, this insignia and motto was in use by VF–21, which continues its use today, flying F–14 Tomcats.

VF–22

The VF–22 insignia (plate 10A) appears in the March 1947 issue of *Naval Aviation News* as VF–22–A, with the coloring of the star reversed. The VF–22 insignia (minus the aircraft) reappears in the January 1954 issue as part of a CAG–4 grouping of five designs, from aboard USS *Lake Champlain*.

VF–24

This insignia (plate 10G) appeared in Sept. 1952 and August 1950 issues of *Naval Aviation News*, which said,

The great Felix, who has survived for half a century and is the only insignia so popular that it got involved in a formal custody battle between squadrons. NAVAIR Archives

"The scimitar stands for eagerness and readiness for battle; the eye-patch, the close scrapes weathered." Another VF–24 patch is shown on plate 5A.

VF–31 "Tomcatters"

No list of the most famous, popular and recognizable Navy insignia would be complete without jaunty Felix the Cat, symbol of the VF–31 "Tomcatters" (plate 5A).

For more than a half-century, Felix has been where the action is. He was on aircraft on board USS *Langley* (CV–1), on USS *Enterprise* at Pearl Harbor (they engaged some attacking planes 200 miles west of Oahu), and on aircraft at Wake Island, Midway Island, Guadalcanal and the Eastern Solomons. Felix was mascot of VF–6 on board USS *Hornet* when Doolittle's B–25s raided Tokyo in April 1943. The squadron has a photo of Charles Lindbergh in an F4B–4 that has Felix painted on the tail. Felix accompanied Butch O'Hare and many others into battle. The emblem appeared on MiG killers in Korea (Ensign F. C. Weber shot down a MiG–15 on Nov. 18, 1950) and Vietnam.

One source dates this familiar insignia back to 1928. However, an article in *Naval Aviation News* in December 1952 noted, "Out of the many hundreds of insignia used during the war, a few Navy and Marine squadrons still keep the old-time emblems of past glory and carry on the traditions. Two appear to be the oldest still in use today—VMF–231's Ace of Spades insignia and VF–31's Felix the Cat. Both were conceived in 1921. VMF–231 is an Akron Reserve outfit and VF–31 is aboard the Leyte."

"History of the Felix emblem is somewhat jumbled in the files of CNO," the article continued. "Back in 1921 Combat Squadron Four was formed and Felix was adopted at that time. Then next year it was disbanded . . . In 1923, Felix bobbed up again with VF–2 . . ." The squadron was redesignated VF–6 in 1927, VB–2 in 1928, VF–3 in 1937 on the *Saratoga*, VF–6 in 1943 and finally VF–31 in 1948.

The 1978 version of the command history calls the 1923 squadron VF–1B, incidentally.

A 1938 explanation of Felix's origins explains that Fighting Plane Squadron 3 (VF–3) adopted its insignia when its primary mission was considered to be the dive-bombing attack. "This mission was clearly pictured by Pat Sullivan's 'Felix' . . . Although the mission of the squadron is now that of fighting, 'Felix' with his bomb had so endeared himself to the personnel that he has been retained." Back then, the colors of the insignia were black and white.

In 1958, *Naval Aviation News* added more tidbits of information to the Felix saga: "'Felix hasn't changed much in 26 years except for the addition of the yellow background and his new *Tomcatters* squadron nickname,' commented VAdm. Charles R. Brown while visiting an old squadron of his." He visited VF–31 aboard USS *Saratoga*; he'd been in the squadron when it was VF–1B, the "Felix the Cat" squadron, on the old *Saratoga* in 1932. "As a squadron insigne, Felix dates back to 1926," the article continued.

Several months later, this article was followed by a letter from another vice admiral, who said he was in the "Felix" Squadron from January 1927 to June 1929. According to his album, he recalls the designation was VF–6 in 1927, and then VB–2–B at the end of their 1927 cruise. "It was at the end of this cruise that Emil Chourre designed the Felix Cat insignia to conform to the new fighter-bomber designation. I believe that VF–1 assumed the 'High Hat' insignia about this time also . . . The 1929 cruise to Panama was the occasion for Lindbergh's visit to the Saratoga while he was in Panama surveying PanAm air routes . . . On my return to the squadron in 1932, the designation had reverted to VF–6 . . . "

In the NAVAIR archives is an issue of *Plane Talk of USS Saratoga*, dated "At sea, January, 1928." One article mentions VB–2B, Light Bombing Squadron 2. The insignia on these planes was a Felix cat with a lighted bomb between his forepaws, the "significance of the insignia being to distinguish planes of Squadron VB–2B as bombing planes."

Felix is unique in that he was once involved in a famous custody battle between a pair of squadrons. In July 1944, VF–6 was ordered to switch designations from VF–6 to VF–3, and, thinking that the squadron that had owned Felix (the old VF–3) had been disestablished, they abandoned their original Shooting Stars insignia in favor of Felix. However, the old VF–3 hadn't been disestablished—it had been redesignated VF–6, and had retained Felix. The Chief of Naval Operations finally had to settle the dispute in July 1946; he disestablished VF–6.

Eagle-eyed insignia buffs and historians will note that the 1929 version of Felix does not picture him in a circle. Also, up through World War II, the fuse on Felix's bomb was not "lit." A 1958 photo shows sparks coming from the fuse.

In the mid 1970s, the members of VF–31 had an unofficial insignia drawn showing Felix carrying a lobster instead of a bomb, because they were hauling so many crustaceans back from Maine.

VF–32 "Swordsmen"

According to one source, this insignia (plate 5A) was designed around the time that VBF–3 was established in early 1945. The sword in the lion's paw was added much later, apparently to make a connection with the squadron nickname. Plate 10I shows the earlier version.

This squadron is based at NAS Oceana and deploys aboard USS *John F. Kennedy*. Squadron members sometimes refer to themselves as "Gypsies," because that is their callsign.

Note that Felix is trailed by a small cloud of dust on this biplane, a Boeing F4B-2, then flown by VF-6B, circa 1930. NAVAIR Archives

VF-33 "Tarsiers" and "Starfighters"

The squadron was established in 1943. It flew Hellcats in the Solomons and provided fighter support for Army and Navy bombers. It was disestablished after the war, then recommissioned in October 1948. It deployed to the Caribbean during the Dominican crisis in 1960, and participated in the Cuban blockade in 1962.

In 1959, VF-33 was using an insignia (plate 5A) that showed a tarsier, "a small, ferocious mammal with a fox-like muzzle, which symbolizes deadly strength." The tarsier went through two versions; the first had a round head and was bug-eyed. The second was much more demonic looking, with more pronounced fangs. Oddly enough, the old bug-eyed version began reappearing in the early 1980s. The squadron did away with the tarsier insignia in 1986 or 1987, when further research allegedly showed that the tarsier wasn't quite as ferocious as they had thought. Their new design was based on a large star, to go with the nickname "Starfighters." One recent unofficial version shows the tarsier, but standing in front of a tomcat with the star and a lightning bolt. At last report, small patches showing the old tarsier had reappeared on squadron flight jackets. Three versions appear in plate 5A. The "Starfighters" version is the newest, circa Feb. 1987; both the standing tarsier and the tomcat are unofficial.

VF-33 flies F-14s out of NAS Oceana, Virginia.

VF-41 "Black Aces"

As of 1953, the VF-41 insignia (plate 5B) was an "animated ace of spades . . . loaded with a rocket to hurl after the one he's just let go from his tail hook equipped cloud." It appears in a group along with the Mach Knockers, VF-42's pawn, and VF-61's skull and crossbones.

Three other versions appear on plate 5B. The cloud with the tailhook outline is circa 1951, and the decal is circa 1985. Note the variations in the shape of the cloud-plane, the position of the arm and red stripe and the location of red highlights.

VF-44 "Hornets"

By April 1955, this squadron had a four of hearts and a four of clubs to symbolize the numbers in their designation (plate 5B).

A different VF-44 insignia (plate 10M) appeared in *Naval Aviation News* in April 1955, strangely enough with the nickname "Banshees" in spite of the word "Hornets" on the patch.

VF-45 "4-and-20 Blackbirds"

This squadron traces its roots back to VT-75, a torpedo squadron that called itself the "Black Knights" and that flew Avengers and Helldivers. It was later redesignated VA-4B, then VA-45 in 1948. The squadron flew 387 combat missions in Korea. It was redesignated VF-45 in October 1985, and received F-16s, making it a full-fledged adversary squadron. See plate 5B.

The squadron history says:
"[The] cocky blackbird, regally attired in tails, sports a green derby and boxing gloves which represent the squadron's potential punch. The blackbird was selected because of its recognized persistence and vigorous nature in attacking and outwitting its enemies, and because it displays an ever-ready and aggressive gleam in its eye." Green was one of the original squadron colors— green was given to the fifth (for attack) squadron of a carrier air group. "The 'four and twenty' recalls the original four regular and 20 reserve pilots in the squadron, while the shredded and smoldering cigar represents the fact that most of the pilots were older and more expe-

In the days of more liberal fuselage markings, Felix showed up on this VF-31 jet. In the cockpit is a squadron visitor, Vice Adm. Charles Brown, then Commander Sixth Fleet, who knew Felix's squadron as VF-1B on USS Saratoga *(CV-3) in the early 1930s. This photo appeared in* Naval Aviation News *in 1958. Naval Aviation News*

This spooky tarsier face figured into the insignia of VF-33 in 1949. The depiction of this creature was later altered, and then finally discarded altogether. NAVAIR Archives

Plate 5A.
VF–1, VF–2, VF–11, VF–16–A, VF–31, VF–14, VF–24, VF–21,
VF–32, VF–33 (three versions)

rienced than those who usually comprised such a squadron. The addition of spats, and the yellow-bordered red star which symbolizes the squadron's adversary mission . . ."

Naval Aviation News, February 1954, says the squadron was aboard USS *Lake Champlain* during Korea: "'When we first landed on board the Lake Champlain,' wrote Ltjg. George Kinnear, who was one of the insigne designers, 'there wasn't a man on the flight deck who didn't get a chuckle out of my unique appearance.' Kinnear reported aboard with his crash helmet topped by a brilliant green derby!"

"'By popular vote, the blackbird was selected over two others,' said Kinnear. 'Boxing gloves were suggested by an enlisted man, Charles G. Mitchell, a personnelman third class. My contribution was the green derby. I picked it up one night as I was returning to the ship from a party in Genoa, Italy. I was riding in a horse-drawn cab and got the crazy idea to ask the driver if I could wear his derby and drive the cab. He agreed, and the minute I perched the bowler on top of my head, I wanted it for my own. After some haggling, the driver finally agreed to let me have it for 700 lira, slightly more than a dollar.' Back at the squadron, they painted it and attached it to a helmet. They decided that the actual helmet with derby attached would be worn only when the pilots reported to or were

The May 1953 issue of Naval Aviation News *showed this group of well-known insignia. Although designations have changed, four of the five are still in active use, and the fifth (the VF-41 ace of spades) is now just a flat card, not an animated one. VA-25 is now VA-65, VF-84 is using the Jolly Roger, VF-43 is using the mailed fist (minus the broken "MACH" banner) and VF-42 has become VA-42.* Naval Aviation News

detached from duty aboard one of the carriers. Three months later the outside world received its first glimpse of the new addition as the squadron prepared to leave the Oriskany for Jacksonville. When the derby-topped helmet popped into view as Kinnear boarded his plane, the surprised ship's band swung into the tune 'Bye, Bye, Blackbirds.'"

VF-51 "Screaming Eagles"

In February 1952, *Naval Aviation News* showed an insignia for this squadron that is a crouching panther, paws on a Japanese sun. The squadron was the first Navy squadron to get jet fighters, receiving its FJ-1s in November 1947. It was also the first Navy squadron to fly combat in Korea; it launched strikes on Pyongyang on July 3, 1950, a few days after the North Koreans invaded the South. VF-51 now uses the well-known Screaming Eagle design (plate 5B) which dates back to 1927 (when it was used by VF-3S). Other designations for that squadron were VF-3B and VF-5B. When that squadron was disestablished, the insignia was adopted by VF-1 (later VF-5), VF-5A and finally VF-51 (in 1948). Astronaut Neil Armstrong, who was shot down in Korea, was a member of this squadron.

VF-66

Circa 1958, VF-66 was using a striding rooster holding a smoking machine gun. The insignia (plate 6B) is now used by the VA-66 "Waldos."

VF-71

This squadron was disestablished in March, 1959 (plate 5C).

VF-74 "Be-Devilers"

Circa 1959, this squadron was using the current "Be-Devilers" insignia (plate 5C), a blue devil looking through a sight. VF-74 is stationed at NAS Oceana. They fly F-14s and deploy aboard the USS *Saratoga*.

VF-82

In 1953, VF-82's insignia had a robot and the slogan "Iron Men" on a cloud. An earlier version (plate 10A) consists of a skull above crossed machine guns.

VF-84 "Jolly Rogers"

This classic, no-nonsense logo and nickname were used by VF-17 during World War II. That squadron had chosen the insignia by 1944; they were also known as "Blackburn's Irregulars" (after the founding squadron skipper) and the "Bearded Pirates." The logo appeared in the June 1946 issue of *Naval Aviation News*, on a flag-shaped field.

One account of the derivation goes back to April 1945, when an ensign named Jack Ernie was flying from USS *Bunker Hill*, and was lost during the invasion of Okinawa. His final transmission was "Remember me with the Jolly Rogers." The squadron was disestablished in 1953.

Plates 5B.
VF–41, VF–45, VF–73, VF–41 (three versions), VF–43, VF–43,
VF–44, VF–51, VF–53, VF–53

Plates 5C.
VF–84 (three versions), VF–54, VF–62, VF–74, VF–71, VF–194,
VF–103, VF(N)–104

VF–84 was established in 1955 at NAS Oceana, Virginia Beach, Virginia, as the "Vagabonds," and took over the famed Jolly Rogers insignia in the late 1950s. When a member of VF–84 was researching squadron roots years later, members of Ensign Ernie's family told them the story; the family reportedly had had the deceased ensign's skull and femurs encased in glass and gave them to the squadron. His name remains on the squadron duty roster, and his skull and bones travel with the squadron as a symbol of courage.

At one point early in the Cold War, the Soviet newspaper *Pravda* took to referring to American pilots as pirates. Analysts were puzzled, until they made the connection with the skull and crossbones insignia of Fighter Squadron 84 (the "Jolly Rogers").

The lineage of this insignia is puzzling. In a December 1957 photo in *Naval Aviation News*, Cdr. Joseph Lovington, "skipper of Fighter Squadron 61, leads his hard hitting team of pilots that flies the 'Jolly Roger.'" In the photo, he is looking at a flag bearing the insignia and the words "Jolly Roger" stenciled at the top. However, a squadron designated VF–61 is not in the lineage of VF–84. Three versions of the Jolly Roger are shown on plate 5C. Note variations on banner, eyes on skull, detail on crossed bones. Old felt patch says "Jolly Rogers" in crude stick letters, with crossed bones shaped like bombs.

VF–101 "Grim Reapers"

The original "Grim Reapers" were established as Fighter Squadron 10 in June 1942, and deployed aboard USS *Enterprise* to the South Pacific. By the time the war was only two-thirds over, the squadron had already racked up forty-three kills in its F4F Wildcats and another eighty-eight flying F6F Hellcats.

This version of the familiar Jolly Roger was in the second group of insignia published by Naval Aviation News, *back in June 1946. Note the flag-shaped design. The skull isn't as forbidding as later versions (it lacks the large crack, for example).* NAVAIR Archives

This insignia was approved for use by VF–84 in April 1960, but it had previously been used by VF–61 and other squadrons. The basic design was originally approved in June 1943, as the insignia of VF–17. NAVAIR Archives

VF–82's insignia, circa the early 1950s. NAVAIR Archives

A third-class petty officer named Jordan, a member of VF-17, cheerfully spray paints kill markings. Note that the squadron's numerical designation is painted out in this old photograph, the work of wartime censors.

The Jolly Roger decorated these Corsairs, flown by VF-17 in 1944. The squadron shot down 154 Japanese planes during 76 days of combat flying near Bougainville and Rabaul, in the Solomon Islands. Lt. Ike Kepford accounted for 16 of those kills. Naval Aviation News

Peter Mersky, in his book *The Grim Reapers—Fighting Squadron Ten in World War II*, gives an excellent explanation of the origin of this insignia (plate 5D):

"While he attended to the administrative details of forming his squadron, Lieutenant Commander Flatley gave thought to a title and emblem for VF–10. He had come up with the name 'Grim Reapers.' While talking to war correspondent Stanley Johnston, who would write a mid-war biography VF–10 and who had been aboard Lexington during the Coral Sea engagement, Flatley discussed the insignia. In his book, Johnston takes credit for the initial idea and sketch of the Grim Reaper skeleton which Flatley eventually turned over to an enlisted artist, Joe Wilkes. Wilkes returned a more finished drawing and painted the new insignia on a 8–foot by 6–foot piece of sailcloth. Flatley proudly displayed the banner behind him in San Diego as he interviewed applicants [for the squadron]."

Johnston, incidentally, was later nearly tried for treason when he leaked a story that American intelligence experts had broken the Japanese codes.

The skeleton is called Old Moe. In a May 1942

CDR. JOSEPH *A. Lovington, CO of Fighter Squadron 61 aboard Saratoga, leads his hard hitting team of pilots that flies the "Jolly Roger."*

As shown in the December 1957 issue of Naval Aviation News, *VF–61 had their Jolly Roger made into a banner on a cruise aboard USS Saratoga.* Naval Aviation News

This old Jolly Roger patch is about as salty as they get—all the black background seems to be worn off. However, its active days are over. It is sewn on a jacket that stays in a collector's closet.

photo, Moe is wearing a flight helmet and goggles; later versions have only goggles. The original banner showed Moe 45 degrees nose down to the right. The current version shows him flying level.

Countess Alexa Zabriskie, who lived on Maui during the war, became well known for adopting a series of Navy squadrons. In September 1942, she "took VF-10 under her wing" and "printed Grim Reaper stationery with the 'Old Moe' insignia" on it.

The rules for painting Old Moe as an aircraft tail marking change regularly. The squadron has either a black-and-white or a red-and-white version on its aircraft, but no multi-color ones. "I think the aircraft are supposed to look dull and drab when they're on the carrier," a recent squadron public affairs officer observed.

A fascinating set of correspondence is in the VF-101 files at the Naval Air History and Archives section at the Washington Navy Yard. It started in July 1952, when the CO of VF-101 (which was established two months earlier) wrote to CNO asking for permission to adopt the insignia that was used by VF-10 during World War II— "the privilege of maintaining the traditions of this famous squadron," he wrote. He suggested the nickname "Grim

Reapers IV," since " 'Grim Reapers III' was the nickname of the third and most recent Fighter Squadron Ten."

The CNO forwarded the request to the Heraldic Branch of the Army's Quartermaster General, noting that the old VF-10 design "does not conform to the provisions" of OPNAV Instruction 5030.4, and asking the Heraldic Branch to create an insignia "incorporating the ideas expressed" in the older version.

In September, the Heraldic Branch's Research and Development Division returned its suggested design, "with the skeleton or specter removed to conform to established policy." The new insignia featured a winged scythe, edged with flame, on a blue disk in front of a red disk. "The inflamed and winged scythe against a series of widening circles symbolizes the keenness and firepower of Fighter Squadron One Hundred One in destroying enemy aircraft, both airborne and at the bases." This design was forwarded to VF-101, "approved as the official insignia for your command, subject to your concurrence."

In December, the skipper of VF-101 went back up the chain, reporting that the new design was "unsatisfactory" for several reasons, including the fact that the

The Grim Reaper insignia makes a perfect backdrop—the VF-10 Reapers were truly mowing 'em down back in May 1942 when they took a break from combat to pose for this photo. They were flying F4F

Wildcats from USS Enterprise *(CV-6). The squadron skipper, Cdr. Jimmy Flatley, is fifth from left in the front row.*

Subtle and not-so-subtle variations appear in this assortment collected by Dave Parsons during his tour with VF-102. Note "Diamondbacks" spelled as both one and two words, differences in banner and details of globe that the snake surrounds.

design's "only resemblance to the original insignia lies in the presence of the scythe" and that the "wings are silver ones, indicative of the U.S. Air Force not Naval Aviation." He cited a provision in the OPNAV that said "the use of existing insignia of famous decommissioned units shall be encouraged," and reiterated the squadron's desire to have Old Moe in light of the "important morale factors inherent in the question."

Two weeks later, the verdict came back: "No objections are interposed to this request which is hereby approved."

VF-102 "Diamondbacks"

Their insignia is a snake encircling a globe. A letter from the Chief of Naval Operations to the squadron skipper in April 1985 is an example of formal approval of an insignia design. The subject line said "Naval Aviation Insignia Approval," reference was to OPNAVINST 5030.4D. The letter said: "Historical records indicate that the insignia currently in use by VF-102 has not been previously approved. The records show that [the design] has been used unofficially since or soon after establishment of the squadron in 1955. In view of its continued use and conformance to the design requirements [of the OPNAV, the design] is hereby approved as the official insignia of VF-102."

VF-103 "Sluggers"

From 1959, this insignia is a lightning bolt through a shamrock, superimposed over a baseball bat. It was established at Cecil Field, Florida, in May 1952, and later at NAS Oceana in July 1965. The Sluggers still fly out of Oceana. See plate 5C.

VF(N)-104

The cat on the buzzsaw (plate 5C) didn't last long; the squadron was disestablished August 1944.

VF-111 "Sundowners"

Established in October 1942 as VF-11. From 1943 to 1945, the original "Sundowners" squadron was credited with 157 destroyed enemy aircraft (fifty-six from April to July 1943). It was redesignated VF-111 in 1948. At the start of the Korean War, a squadron member scored the first Navy jet kill. The squadron also made seven Vietnam cruises, collecting two kills, a MiG-21 and a MiG-17.

The logo was designed in late 1942 while the unit was stationed in Hawaii. They were "adopted" by a Maui couple, Boyd and Maria von Tempsky, who owned a large cattle ranch. The pilots decided VF-11 should have an insignia, and they devised the concept of two Wildcats shooting a rising sun into the ocean as symbolic of their mission.

A lieutenant in the squadron, who was later to retire as a rear admiral, recalled, "We fancied ourselves able to down the Japanese son of destiny, or Japanese sons borne on aircraft wings, or whatever we encountered." With the help of Boyd's sister Alexa, the insignia was rendered in color, and each F4F was stenciled with the emblem. At that time numerals were not allowed on unit insignia but along the bottom was printed "Sundowners." The term sundowner also refers to a strict, hardworking

The 1956 version of the famous Sundowner insignia. NAVAIR Archives

This patch version of the VF-53 design features the squadron nickname. NAVAIR Archives

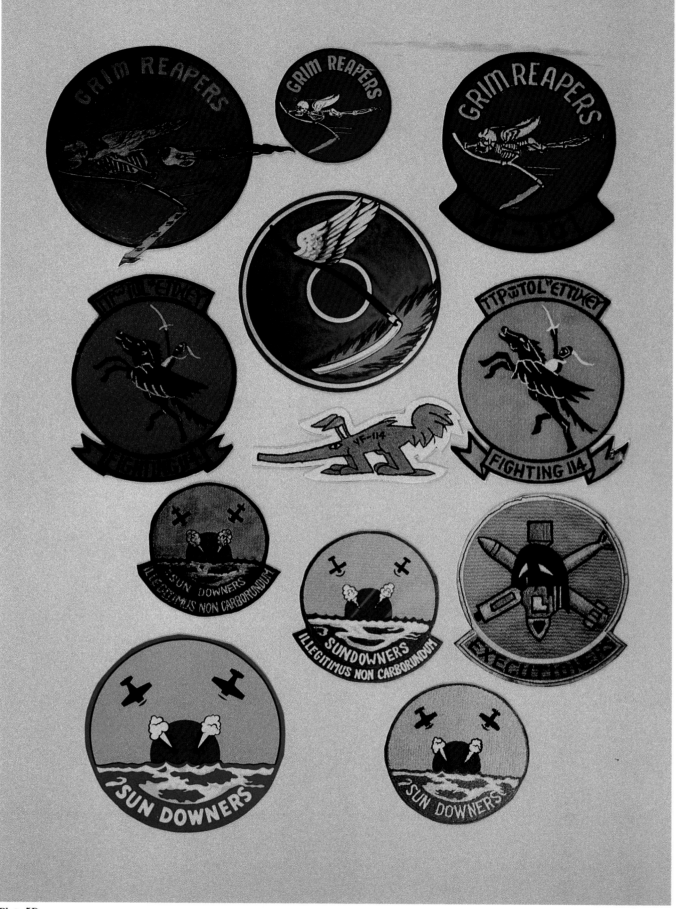

Plate 5D.
VF–101 (three versions), VF–114, VF–101, VF–114, VF–114, VF–111
(four versions), VF–114

captain who wouldn't allow grog until after dark, instead of the usual ration allotted when the sun dipped below the yardarm. The term stayed in use long after liquor was banished from Navy ships.

The "Sundowners" were withdrawn from combat in July 1943, and returned in October aboard USS *Hornet*. According to a *Naval Aviation News* article by historian and writer Barrett Tillman, "Security measures had tightened and, during the *Hornet* tour that ended in January 1945, the squadron's F6F Hellcats did not sport the Sundowner emblem. The F4Fs disappeared from the insignia shortly after VF–11 entered the jet age . . . To mark the transition from props to jets, the Wildcats were replaced in the insignia by Panthers . . . As time went on, a growing awareness of the squadron's traditions prompted a return of the Wildcats in the insignia. In some renditions, the aircraft only vaguely resembled F4Fs, but at least they were unmistakably prop-driven instead of jet propelled."

During the Vietnam era, the phrase *Illegitimus Non Carborundum* (Don't Let the Bastards Grind You Down) was added beneath the insignia.

Variations in the spelling of "Sundowners" (as one or two words), have occurred during the years, as well as differences in the shape of the aircraft and the pattern on the water (plate 5D). The Sundowners are currently stationed at NAS Miramar, California and fly F–14s.

VF–113 "Stingers"

In *Naval Aviation News*, August 1950, the insignia shows a bee with a pointed tail, against a hive-shaped background, with "Stingers" written at the bottom. The "bumblebee signified its fighter planes; the stinger, their 20 mm. cannon." The "Stingers" patch in plate 7H dates back to 1950; the insignia is currently used by VFA–113.

VF–114 "Executioners" and "Aardvarks"

The genesis and lineage of this squadron's insignia are among the most tangled and confusing of all. Tracking down the who-what-when-where part can be like a mystery story, except you don't have all the clues and you sometimes don't find out "whodunit."

A letter from the Aviation History Unit in 1965 tried to set the squadron lineage straight. According to the Unit's official research, the squadron began as VBF–19 in January 1945, using an insignia of a diving stork firing four guns and delivering a rocket, with Mt. Fuji in the background. This design was replaced by a flaming winged sword in the late 1940s, and (in 1950) a black executioner's mask superimposed over a crossed gun, bomb and rocket (plate 5D). The squadron nickname was "Executioners."

Everything seems straightforward so far—a clear lineage for the squadron, and a classic, gutsy, fighter-type insignia and nickname. Time for things to get tangled up.

In 1951, the Commander Air Force, Pacific Fleet, wrote a letter to the squadron, saying, "Although the insignia is already approved, it is considered to be inappropriate." The letter listed several reasons, including the fact that the word "Executioners" had what the letter called "an unsavory connotation which appears to reflect discredit to the Navy and does not indicate any degree of valor." The letter continues, "The 'Motto' also provides excellent propaganda for the enemy [like that] effectively used by the Germans during the last war when it became known that one Air Force unit was using the motto 'Murder Inc.' It is recalled that the American public became considerably agitated as a result and caused the unit to refrain from using the expression or placing it on their aircraft." "Persuaders" was suggested as an alternative nickname; the record doesn't show an alternative insignia.

Nor does the official history file show that the Executioner went away. In spite of the official arm-twisting in the 1951 letter, the former nickname remained in use into the early 1960s. The next event in the saga was in 1961, according to a story published in *The Hook* magazine, when the squadron skipper became dissatisfied with the "Executioner" insignia. He had the squadron public affairs officer research the squadron history, and (erroneously) traced the squadron's lineage back to VB–2, which had the Pegasus-Bellerophon motif.

The squadron members voted to keep the old Executions insignia, but "the CO called for another vote, cast his 51%, counted the ballots himself, thanked us warmly for our unflagging command support," the article said. "At the peon level, there was a decided lack of enthusiasm," since the squadron felt their wishes were ignored. Casting about for an alternative, "Some ready room sage noted that the Aardvark was the first varmint in the dictionary and we were the first Phantom squadron." So they chose the aardvark as an unofficial symbol (plate 5D), and began using it in an underground manner.

In 1962, the squadron got approval to change to the old Pegasus-Bellerophon insignia, which has quite a history itself. That insignia is credited to VB–5B, which had submitted it for approval in December 1934. That earlier squadron used it until it was disestablished in July 1942; it was then adopted by Bombing Squadron 11, later designated VA–11A and VA–114, until it was disestablished in December 1949.

In the original design, Bellerophon rode Pegasus in a dive to depict the squadron's bombing mission. In the new VF–114 version, the heraldry was rotated 90 degrees clockwise, putting the horse and rider in a climb to symbolize the change from dive-bombing to an interceptor role. The resulting insignia shows Bellerophon, nose high to the left. Also, Bellerophon is holding a sword instead of a bomb. This version was officially approved in June 1962.

Meanwhile, the aardvark (plate 5D) became extremely popular, probably because of its grass-roots origin. A 1963 article in *Naval Aviation News* says the squadron "acquired the nickname when this character began appearing on squadron gear, correspondence, etc. The squadron adopted the mythical mascot with permission of its creator, John Hart, the author of the syndicated comic strip 'B.C.'"

Today, some of the squadron's aircrews wear orange

Plate 5E.
VF–126, VF–142, VF–126, VF–152, VF–143, VF–143, VF–151,
VF–144, VF–151, VF–151, VF–154

flight suits, which have long been out of the supply system but that are carefully handed down from crew to crew, matching the color of the aardvark on the insignia.

VF–141 "Iron Angels"

In *Naval Aviation News*, January 1954, an article said "VF-141 has dropped its old squadron insignia and adopted that used by VF-14 during World War II [plate 10A]. The new insignia of the Iron Angels features an armor-clad knight carrying a .50 cal machine gun. A halo and pair of wings completes the angel theme. VF-141 formerly used Woody Woodpecker astride a Panther jet, in the act of impaling a star. The squadron's name then was the Starbusters."

This member of the VF-142 "Ghostriders" opted for wearing his nylon flight jacket instead of the leather G-1 at an air show in Mildenhall, England, in 1984. Most aviators seem to have strong preferences about which type of jacket is their favorite. Robert F. Dorr

VF–142 "Ghostriders"

This squadron was established at NAS Alameda, California, as VF-193 in 1948. They served seven combat deployments in Vietnam, scoring five aerial victories. VF-142 flies the F-14 out of NAS Oceana and deploys aboard the USS *Eisenhower*. See plate 5E.

VF–143 "Pukin' Dogs"

This insignia dates back to at least 1949. The Latin motto reads "Sans Reproache," but the universal nickname is the Pukin' Dogs. The creature on the insignia is supposed to be a griffin, a mythological beast with the body of a lion, and the head and wings of an eagle. The griffin "implies a vigilant or repellant guardian," according to one 1940 era description of insignia. The story goes that when the skipper's wife first saw it, she said, "That doesn't look like a griffin, it looks like a dog throwing up." The pilots loved it. A life-size, carved wooden pukin' dog is in the squadron's ready room.

The first appearance of the design was in *Naval Aviation News* in March 1950. The griffin faces to the left, instead of the right. The slogan "Sans Reproache" is just beneath its feet and inside the chevron-shaped field of the insignia. There are four white stripes at the top of the field. The caption says the creature is "a winged black panther ready to strike a foe." In 1953, the logo appeared in photos of Fighter Squadron 53. Then called the "Blue Knights," their patch was shield-shaped, with a light background and the griffin facing left.

By 1966, however, the creature was facing right.

The ancestor of the insignia that (facing in the other direction) today's Pukin' Dogs of VF-143 would make famous. Naval Aviation News

VF-171 chose these playing cards to spell out their designation. The skeleton is robed like the Grim Reaper. NAVAIR Archives

Pranksters from a rival fighter squadron once stole a statue of the Pukin' Dog belonging to VF-143, posed it with a VF-102 hat beside one of the "Diamondback's" aircraft and sent humorous ransom notes to the owners.

There are three stripes at the top, and "Fighting-143" in the banner at the bottom. See plate 5E.

VF-144 "Bitter Birds"

One version of this insignia (plate 10N) shows an angry Kansas Jayhawk carrying a large club with a nail through it, with the slogan "Bitter Birds" underneath. Under the designation VF-884, this squadron operated off the USS *Boxer* in Korea. This squadron is in the lineage of the current VA-52 "Knightriders," who use a different insignia. Another VF-144 patch is shown on plate 5E.

VF-154 "Black Knights"

Milton Caniff drew their current insignia in 1957, from a design by John "Crash" Miottel, Jr., a former member of the squadron. It shows a knight in armor, standing with a shield. VF-154 now flies F-14s out of NAS Miramar. See plate 5E.

VF-171 "Aces"

This squadron was originally established as VF-82 at NAS Atlantic City, Apr. 1, 1944. VF-171 was deployed on the USS *Bennington* (CV-20) for World War II combat operations in the Pacific, and participated in the first carrier strikes on Tokyo. It was the first Navy jet squadron, getting the FD-1 Phantom in July 1947, and was disestablished in March 1958. Squadron history says it was "recommissioned 8 August 1977," although the official Navy history branch does not recognize or approve this term. When VF-101 traded its F-4s for F-14s at that time, VF-171 was created as the F-4 FRS (Fleet Replacement Squadron). The skipper of the new squadron liked an old VF-82 "Aces" insignia (plate 5F) and adopted it for his new outfit, giving rise to the "recommissioned" misconception. This squadron has since been disestablished.

VF-174

Circa 1953, this squadron used the old VB-81 "Hell Razors" insignia (plate 6D). VF-174 became VA-174 in July 1966.

VF-194 "Red Lightning"

Like VF-191, this squadron's existence was brief. Their insignia showed a lightning bolt through an ace of hearts, (plate 5C) with "Red Lightning" written above and "Dictum Factum" beneath. The insignia was derived from that of VF-91, circa 1955.

The tail marking used by VF-194 during its rather brief existence. The insignia was derived from that of VF-91, circa 1955. NAVAIR Archives

Plate 5F.
VF-161, VF-162, VF-171, VF-191, VF-173, VF-202, VF-211,
VF-201, VF-703, VF-211, VF-213, VF-301

Chapter 6

Attack squadrons

As in the chapter about fighter squadrons, the following selection of attack squadrons represents only a small portion of the historical roster, and only part of those illustrated in the color plates in this book. Attack squadron insignia, as a rule, are slightly less morbid and bloodthirsty than those of fighter squadrons, although plenty of weapons and warlike symbols appear. Cartoon figures and animals are common on attack insignia, along with numerous iterations of the riding-the-bomb motif.

Although the basic, kudo-packed squadron history isn't too hard to come by, information about the birth and genesis of a particular insignia design is almost impossible to find. When research has established unlikely links between designs, or anecdotes about the origin of an insignia, that squadron has been included.

At times in various squadron lineages, attack squadrons have turned into fighter squadrons, and vice versa. An entry may appear for an attack squadron that later became a fighter squadron; thus, some insignia have been shared by both a fighter and an attack squadron.

Included are VAH squadrons, the so-called "heavy attack" designations, abbreviated as HATRON on some patches. Those squadrons flew A–3 Skywarriors and RA–5 Vigilantes.

VAH–7 "Peacemakers"
Circa 1962, the insignia showed two upright pistols (plate 10O). The insignia of a different VAH–7 (plate 10O) was also shown as being in use by VC–7 in the Dec. 1952 issue of *National Aviation News*.

VAH–9 "Hoot Owls"
In late 1960, this squadron was using a stylized owl face (plate 10O) over crossed lightning bolts, a cloud and a bomb. The design reappeared in print in 1968, when the squadron was designated as a Reconnaissance Attack Squadron.

VA–12 "Flying Ubangis"
This squadron was originally established in May 1945 as VBF–4. It received its designation as an attack squadron in August 1948, and transferred to NAS Cecil Field, Florida, in February 1949, their home ever since. It became VA–12 in 1955. According to the squadron his-

VA–12 took advantage of the pre-Tactical Paint Scheme rules to get their "Kiss of Death" tail marking airborne.

Plate 6A.
VA–22, VA–23, VA–27, VA–36, VA–35, VA–34, VA–36, VA–35,
VA–37, VA–42, VA–45, VA–46

tory, "the 'Kiss of Death' has appeared upon each of the seven different types of aircraft flown by the Ubangis and has become world famous while flying from 12 different carriers . . ."

Nevertheless, the provenance of the nickname and the insignia is muddled. In December 1952, *Naval Aviation News* said the "Kiss of Death" squadron was VF–13. The "Kiss of Death" design first appeared in print in September 1949, when it was adopted by VF–12, which explained, "it was desired to have the observer of the insignia left with the impression that the kiss of death is coming his way, and he can kiss this world good-bye."

VA–12 once used an insignia that showed a cartoon native with a bone through his nose. John Parker, a "graphic arts mechanic" in the decal shop at NAD Norfolk, remembers the Ubangi native from the 1950s. Parker said the ship cruised "to Africa and those people didn't appreciate it. It wasn't exactly a goodwill gesture." The jet rework facility has a bone-through-the-nose guy on the wall that bears the legends "PATRON 5" and "The Savage Sons."

VA–23 "Black Knights"

The insignia says "In Omnia Paratus," and shows (plate 6A and plate 10I) a shield with helmet at top (circa 1966).

VA–34 "Blue Blasters"

This squadron was established as VF–20 in October 1943. It entered World War II aboard USS *Lexington* (CV–16), and saw action at Manila, Luzon, Mindoro and Formosa. The squadron was redesignated VF–9A in

November 1946, and later VF–91 (1948), VF–34 (1950) and finally VA–34 in October 1956. "At NAS Cecil Field, Florida, on June 1 [1969], just four months short of 26 years of continuous service, Attack Squadron 34 was disestablished," a squadron history said. The current squadron says it was recommissioned in January 1970, although that is a disputed concept and term. The squadron flies the A–6, based at NAS Oceana, Virginia.

One of VF–20's original insignia showed a joker tearing through a deck of cards, holding a machine gun. This insignia reflected the squadron's nickname, "Jokers Coming Through." A 1944 note from Fighting Squadron 20 said, "In this area, young, 'new' pilots are customarily addressed and referred to as 'JOKERS.' The youngsters in this squadron accepted the challenging designation; 'O.K., watch the JOKERS COME THRU!' They are."

Another early insignia showed bomb blasts on a blue background. The 1945 version showed a frontal view of a skull, with a tiny skeleton Landing Signal Officer (LSO) holding paddles for eyes, and "Fighting 20" for teeth. This LSO signal is called "roger ball" and means a smooth approach to the carrier's flight deck. In the mid 1960s, the insignia (plate 6A) evolved to a partial side view of the skull, now bearing a machine-gun cigarette holder and eagle wings. Roy Crane, creator of the "Buzz Sawyer" comic strip, designed one of these latter two insignia, but

The earliest version of VA–34's classic insignia. This insignia dates from when they were VF–20. NAVAIR Archives

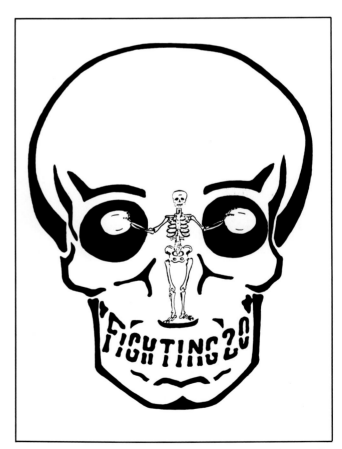

The second incarnation of the current VA–34 insignia, this one also from when the squadron flew fighters. NAVAIR Archives

The current Blue Blaster insignia is one of the true classics: colorful, popular and rich in both heritage and symbolism.

VA-45's jaunty crow decorates the ready-room seats at the squadron's home at NAS Key West, Florida.

accounts vary as to whether it was the 1945 or 1966 version.

Lt. Cdr. Steve O'Sullivan, a squadron member, said, "I've heard people say that they wanted to get into this squadron just so they could wear the patch. There's a squadron over here that has a pawn on its patch—who wants a pawn? I think we've got the neatest one in the whole air wing."

VA-35 "Black Panthers"

Called the "Navy's oldest attack squadron," it was established in July 1934 as VB-3B, "deployed aboard USS Ranger (CV-4) flying the fabric-covered Great Lakes

The familiar "4-and-20" design conjures up World War II graphics in a way that very few current designs manage. (See entry for VF-45 in chapter 5.) Naval Aviation News

Plate 6B.
VA–52, VA–52, VA–55, VA–65, VA–65, VA–72, VA–66, VA–75,
VA–85, VA–76, VA–81, VA–85, VA–86

BG–1 bi-plane . . . Proud of its origins and mission, the squadron adopted the Black Panther as its insignia since it embodies the characteristics of the bombing squadron: namely, stealth, diving, tactics and decisiveness."

A late 1950s version of the insignia says "ATTACK-RON 35" on the banner at the bottom. By July 1968 the banner said, "ATKRON 35." It was then called "the oldest attack squadron and the third oldest carrier squadron in the Navy" in *Naval Aviation News*. See plate 6A. The Black Panthers fly A–6s out of NAS Oceana.

VA–36 "Roadrunners"

The current VA–36 was established in March 1987. Squadron history traces its lineage back to another Attack Squadron 36, that began as VF–102 in May 1952, and that was disestablished in August 1970. An inquiry to the insignia-approving authority asking about the former VA–36 insignia which showed a cartoon roadrunner. This inquiry drew the response that the old VA–36 insignia had never been approved, and that it "would have been disapproved because of its design" because the existing OPNAV "prohibited the use of cartoon portrayals . . . The insignia may be modified to include a realistic bird. However, the figure must not be portrayed as performing human tasks . . . Since nicknames are unofficial, the name 'Roadrunners' may be adopted by the new squadron." They designed a realistic version (plate 6A).

VA–42 "Green Pawns"

One indirect predecessor was established as VBF–74 at NAS Chincoteague, Va. in 1945, and disestablished in June 1950. With the outbreak of hostilities in Korea, a reactivated reserve squadron was designated VF–42, which was later redesignated VA–42. The insignia shows a simple green chess piece on a white field. The squadron is the Atlantic Fleet Replacement Squadron for the A–6.

VA–45

This squadron was established in 1963. A version of its insignia is in plate 6A. In February 1985, it became VF–45 (see entry).

VA–52 "Knight Riders"

Their insignia (plate 6B) shows a knight riding a turtle. It was adopted in September 1959, after the squadron was redesignated VA–52 from VF–144. The squadron's explanation of the design follows:

"The knight portrays the pilots of our aircraft, he is the legendary protector of freedom and honor and exemplifies today's Naval Aviator. The knight is holding a mace, an ancient and foreboding weapon . . . The large sea turtle is the fabled denizen of the sea whose determination, stamina, and navigational abilities are unquestionable . . . The turtle's inclusion in the patch is not meant to indicate lack of speed. Unlike his brother the land tortoise, the sea turtle is a capable and speedy performer when in his element, the sea."

VA–52 currently flies A–6s out of NAS Whidbey Island, Washington.

This early version of the Sunday Punchers insignia was used when the squadron was designated VA-7-A, dating back to 1948. NAVAIR Archives

VA–65 "Fighting Tigers"

This squadron was established in May 1945, when it was named VT–74 and flew Helldivers. The squadron moved to NAS Oceana, Virginia Beach, Virginia, in 1946. It has also been designated VA–2B, VA–25 (1948) and received its current designation in 1959. The squadron flew 1,239 sorties over Vietnam and expended ten million pounds of ordnance. As shown in plate 6B, the insignia is a fierce, advancing tiger. The squadron flies the A–6, and is based at NAS Oceana.

VA–75 "Sunday Punchers"

VA–75 was established July 1943 as VB–18, flying the SBD Douglas Dauntless dive-bomber. A later designation was VA–7A (November 1946); as shown in the July 1948 issue of *Naval Aviation News*, the insignia was then a pugnacious boy wearing boxing gloves and riding on a bomb. The words "Sunday" and "Punchers" appear on his left and right. "The squadron employed the slogan during the recent war," the caption said. The official explanation of this insignia follows:

"[The] small boy in fighting togs riding a bomb constitutes the spirit and aggressiveness of the attack squadron; its constant vigil of defense, its readiness to meet all enemies, and attack any objective. The fighter, drawn as a small boy with a facial expression of determination, a stance of readiness, and fists clenched for action, is meant to signify the feeling of aggression, the fighting spirit . . . The slogan 'Sunday Punchers' is a carry over from the old wartime insignia. It is a slogan that the squadron fought under during World War II, and it was the feeling of every squadron member that it should be kept for that reason . . ."

Later designations included VA–74 (July 1948), and VA–75 (February 1950). A June 1985 information sheet

Plate 6C.
VA–93, VA–93, VA–95, VA–97, VA–104, VA–105, VA–127, VA–115,
VA–145, VA–145

58

The "almost perfect stogie count" dates from the pre-health-conscious days of the Navy, apparently. Whether cigars were par for the course or *the squadron was celebrating something special is unknown.* Naval Aviation News

about VA–75 shows the insignia of a bomb falling through a boxing glove superimposed on a pair of wings, signifying a "hay-maker" punch. However, the block on the form that says "approved" is marked "No." The narrative explains:

VA–76 worked its designation into a patriotic theme (the design includes a musket and a colonial hat). Naval Institute

Aboard USS *John F. Kennedy* in December 1983, on station off Beirut, they launched seven aircraft as part of a retaliatory strike against an antiaircraft artillery (AAA) position that had fired on F–14s the previous day. During the strike, the AAA hit one of their A–6s. The crew had to eject. The pilot died, and the bombardier-navigator, Lt. Bobby Goodman, was taken prisoner.

"This insignia was approved for the original squadron (VB–18) on 14 January 1944. It was discontinued on

The Hell Razors insignia shows up in this collage of Carrier Air Group 81 designs from the late 1940s. The black panther at top is reminiscent of the current insignia of VF–21, which has a similar shield shape, topped by a rampant panther. NAVAIR Archives

Plate 6D.
VA–146, VA–147, VA–152, VA–155, VA–155, VA–174, VA–175,
VA–176, VA–192, VA–304, VA–196

25 January 1944 because the squadron thought it violated instructions of the Air Force Pacific Fleet. However, the Bureau did not disapprove it and it was reapproved 29 May 1945. On 25 June 1947 it was replaced with the boy on a bomb wearing boxing gloves. The use of this boxing glove with wings insignia was never reapproved by the Bureau of Aeronautics and has been in use by the squadron since some time about 1970. The little boy insignia was never transferred from VA–74 to VA–75. Hence VA–75 does not have an official approved insignia at this time (10 June 1985)."

The squadron moved to NAS Oceana in 1957. The current squadron public affairs officer says this insignia is derived form several versions, one of which came from the Disney studios. A trivia note: A flying boxing glove appeared in the insignia of an Air Force squadron, the 320th Fighter Squadron.

VA–85 "Black Falcons"

VA–85 was established in February 1952, moved to Oceana that July and got its current designation as VA–85 in January 1953. During their fourth Vietnam deployment, this one aboard USS *Constellation*, they flew 1,500 missions, dropped twelve million pounds of ordnance and didn't lose an aircrew. The insignia is a stark, stylized bird of prey (plate 6B).

In July 1955, their insignia was an upright winged bomb.

VA–86 "Sidewinders"

In early 1959, this squadron's design (plate 6B) showed a fanged snake coiled around a top hat and cane. The squadron is now VFA–86, flying the F–18 out of NAS Cecil Field, Florida.

VA–93 "Ravens"

Two versions of this squadron's former insignia reveal the subtle differences between the patch version and the decal version of the same design (plate 6C). The current VA–93 insignia shows two very stylized, dart-like aircraft against concentric blue circles (plate 6C).

The ubiquitous spade motif reappears yet again, here on the design of VA–195, circa 1956. The current VA–196 insignia is a close derivative, with a close-up face of the devil, and minus the gun and bomb. NAVAIR Archives

VA–155

This insignia (plate 6D) shows a snake coiled through the eye holes of a skull. According to *Naval Aviation News* in 1949, "The macabre death's head and cobra . . . poised to attack, the snake typifies the sudden death mission of the attack squadron."

VA–174 "Hell Razors"

VA–174 was established as VB–81 in 1944. According to one source, "At that time, famed cartoonist and fine arts designer Walt Disney conceived both the name "Hellrazors" and the squadron's insignia—a strange caricature of an imaginary batlike, razor-beaked creature from hell." It was disestablished in June 1988. See plate 6D.

Chapter 7

Other squadrons

The following squadrons include everything except fighter and attack—squadrons that rarely (and sometimes never) fly the headline-grabbing glory missions, but that are a crucial part of the picture nevertheless. The insignia are a motley assortment, ranging from humorous to stolid, and from clever to obscure. Few have the long, colorful histories associated with squadrons such as the Tophatters and Grim Reapers, although some of the patrol squadron insignia offer striking exceptions.

Squadrons appear when research has uncovered anecdotes of information about the derivation or genesis

Members of Mine Spotting Unit 9 decorate one of their helos with a drawing of Pogo (wearing a propeller beanie, sitting on a floating mine and holding a rescue sling). Helo fuselage decorations have always been rare. They chose Pogo because a sailor on an LST (Landing Ship, Tank) once remarked that only a pogo stick could land and take off from the ship's cramped deck. Dec. 19, 1953. USN

of the insignia. In other cases, squadrons have been included to round out the spectrum of squadron type and insignia design; in other cases, squadrons appear because their insignia make an important point about a trend in design, or simply because the insignia is visually interesting. In all cases, the result is simply a snapshot of the overall tapestry.

Once you move away from fighter squadrons and attack squadrons, designations and abbreviations get increasingly complex. Even when the basic two-letter symbol has remained the same, its meaning has changed, and patches often include other forms of abbreviations besides the two-letter system.

For example, through the years, VS has meant Scouting, Anti-Submarine, Air Anti-Submarine, and Carrier Air Anti-Submarine. Scouting squadrons are long gone, but other variations apparent in the patches (plate 7C) exhibit a wide variety of abbreviations of the squadron type: SEASTRIKRON, AIRASRON, VS, AIRANTISUBRON.

VC has meant both Fleet Composite or Composite, and is also written FLECOMPRON. VAQ has meant Carrier Special, Tactical Electronics Warfare, and Carrier Tactical Electronics Warfare. VFP means Photographic Reconnaissance squadron. VX is the abbreviation for Air Test and Evaluation Squadron. Other V-combination initializations include: VAP (Heavy Photographic Reconnaissance or Photographic Composite), VAW (Carrier Electronic Warfare or Carrier Airborne Early Warning), VJ (General Utility, Reconnaissance, Weather, Photographic), VFP (Light Photographic or Light Photographic Reconnaissance), VR (Transport), VFA (Fighter Attack or Strike), VF(AW) (All-Weather Fighter), VP (Patrol), VPB (Patrol Bomber), VQ (Reconnaissance (also written VFP), VR (Transport), VS (Scouting Plane, Scouting), VT (Torpedo and Bombing, Torpedo, or Training), and VU (Utility, sometimes written UTRON).

Odds and ends that appear on some patch scrolls or in the basic design include CVG (which meant Aircraft Carrier Air Group circa 1944), STRKFITRON (Strike Fighter), FLELOGSUPPRON (Fleet Logistics Support), and TRARON (Training).

Helicopter squadrons have experienced similar alphabetitis, except they're a bit easier to decipher. HELMINERON means Mine Countermeasures; you'll also find HC (Combat Support), HM (Helicopter), HSL (ASW Lamps), HT (Training), HU (Utility—see plate 10F), and

Plate 7A.
VP–1, VP–5, VP–6, VP–8, VP–8, VP–10, VP–16, VP–16, VP–18,
VP–18, VP–19, VP–19

Plate 7B.
VP-24, VF(N)-103, VP-22, VP-21, VP-26, VP-44, VP-40, VP-22,
VP-62, VP-45, VP-40, VP-48, VP-49, VP-46

HELATKRON (Attack). There were also typical, widespread variations in the spellings and abbreviations of HS squadrons (including HELSUPPRON and HSRON), apparent in the patch scrolls on plate 10D. At other times, HS has meant Carrier ASW.

HS-11 "Dragon Slayers"

This insignia (plate 7J) appeared in *Naval Aviation News* in March 1966, when a squadron helo had recently picked up the Gemini 7 crew.

HU-1

This squadron had one of the first helo insignia to appear in the *Naval Aviation News* series, in January 1952. It shows two sailors in a bulbous winged helo, one looking through a telescope, the other tossing out a life ring (plate 10F and 10N). The insignia says "HU-1" (for Helicopter Utility Squadron) at top center, with an anchor in the background. "One of the busiest squadrons in the Korea War," the caption said. "They have rescued hundreds of downed pilots and wounded ground troops. Their latest job was to fly United Nation conferees to peace meets."

VAQ-33 "Firebirds"

Established on May 31, 1949, this squadron started out as the VC-33 "Nighthawks," flying Avengers for antisubmarine warfare. The squadron was with Air Group 2 in Korea. In 1956, its designation switched to VA(AW)-33, an all-weather attack squadron. In 1969, the squadron's career appeared to be drawing to a close, when it was not chosen to transition to the Navy's newest attack aircraft, the A-3 Skywarrior. At that point, the squadron history says, it "began the depressing task of turning its aircraft over to NAS Quonset Point, Rhode Island . . . A last-minute reprieve, however, was granted," and the squadron was redesignated VAQ-33. Insignia appears on plate 7D. VA-185, established in December 1986, uses the old "Nighthawk" nickname.

VAQ-136 "Jammers"

The insignia shows an upright, mailed fist clutching lightning bolts. The squadron's nickname refers to its radar-jamming, electronic warfare role. See plate 7D.

VC-5 "Checkertails"

Established as VU-5, a utility squadron, in April 1950. The squadron retired its old insignia in 1987, using a design "drawn for the first time on a napkin in Taegu, Korea, during Team Spirit 87 . . . The checker board symbolized the history of VC-5 . . . the red star is a reminder of VC-5's adversary role and the arrows represent the squadron's mission of dissimilar air combat maneuvering." See plate 10J.

VC-27

According to a 1950 explanation in *Naval Aviation News*, this squadron, "Bearing the insignia inspired by Leslie Charteris' *Saint*, participated in the invasions of

The insignia of Carrier Air Wing 5, displayed over USS Midway *(CV-41), show a sample collection of squadron types and shifting designations. VFA-192 was VA-192, and VFA-151 was a fighter squadron, for example, although other VFA squadrons still exist. For reference, there is also VAW, VAQ (VAQ-136 is at center left), two regular attack, and HS squadrons. USN*

the Palau Islands, Mindoro Island, Luzon and Subic Bay Peninsula, and performed outstandingly in the Battle for Leyte Gulf. The squadron chose the *Saint* because it typified a force that strikes courageously and effectively against the enemy. The celebrated author of 'whodunits' was happy to have his trademark become a battle device for a combat unit."

The character of the Saint raises an interesting sidelight on aviation insignia and decorations, a trait not usually shared by British pilots. A. E. Cormack, of the Aircraft Department, Royal Air Force Museum, London, had this to say: "As regards badges on flying clothing I can state categorically that RAF pilots did now sew badges on their flying kit during the war with the sole exception of pre-war white coveralls. There are photographs of the early war years '39-'41 both in UK and the Middle East which show squadron badges worn on the breast pocket of white flying suits . . . In more recent times aircrew have worn rank, unit and name tag additions to flying suits both on the upper arms and the chest . . . The only other decoration which did appear from time to time was personal insignia painted or drawn onto life jackets." One photo shows a Battle of Britain participant, a sergeant who has a drawing of the Saint on his life jacket, except that the stick figure is holding a swastika. Other examples provided by Cormack show girls, pinups and cartoons.

VP-5 "Mad Foxes"

VP-5's insignia (plate 7A) depicts a fox smashing submarine periscopes, with palm trees at left and snow-capped mountains at right. Their missions range from "tropics to Arctic" in the Atlantic. The squadron is based at NAS Jacksonville, Florida, flying P-3Cs.

Plate 7C.
VS–21, VS–21, VS–24, VS–30, VS–24, VS–29, VS–31, VS–31,
VS–37, VS–38, VS–41, VS–48, VS–775, VS–916

VP-6

This insignia from the late 1940s shows Popeye riding on the back of an aircraft, shooting bull's eyes through smoke rings with his right hand and holding a torpedo with his left. The image is superimposed over a compass, and there is a small submarine silhouette at the center bottom. A different VP-6, the "Blue Sharks" (plate 7A), now flies the P-3C.

VP-10 "Red Lancers"

This insignia (a descending bomb, radio waves and stars in a compass) dates back to 1930, when it was designed by the original VP-10. The current VP-10 adopted the design (plate 7A) when it was established in 1951. VP-10 currently flies P-3Cs out of NAS Brunswick, Maine.

VP-12 "Black Cats"

VP-12 was the original "Black Cat" squadron. It garnered the nickname in late 1942 when it pioneered night-bombing tactics in the South Pacific, flying Catalinas. One report said, "*Cats* played Santa to the Japanese at Buin on Christmas Eve [1942] with a sockful of torpedos. The holiday spirit was carried over to New Year's Eve when Lt. Norman Pederson, USNR, over Munda, sounded his plane's crew-warning horn exactly at midnight and released a bomb, a flare and two dozen empty beer bottles."

VP-19 "Big Red"

This squadron was established as VPB-907 in 1946. Its current designation was in 1953. An old VP-19 insignia showed a globe with a cloud, a crossed lightning bolt and a mace behind it, and a helmet above. The new emblem (plate 7A) shows a stylized bird of prey sweeping to the left, talon outstretched. It was adopted "sometime between 1974 and 1980," the squadron public affairs officer said. VP-19 currently flies the P-3C out of NAS Moffett Field, California.

VP-24 "Batmen"

Established as VB-104 at NAS Kaneohe, Hawaii in April 1943, the squadron was redesignated VPB-104 the next year. Their insignia is unique in that it is the only officially approved one that depicts that great World War II tradition, the pinup girl (plate 7B). After World War II, this squadron assisted in testing the Navy's first air-to-surface missile, which was called "The Bat," from which the squadron derived its nickname and insignia. The first published appearance of the bat girl insignia was in 1953. Its design includes a parachute mine, sub periscope and cavalry sword.

VP-26 "Tridents"

VP-26 was given its current designation in 1948, although it began five years earlier as VB-114. According to the squadron history, one early insignia was designed in 1958 by "the late Lt. Bockenhauer. The black bat symbolized the Martin P-4 aircraft originally employed

VC-27 adapted the logo of Leslie Charteris's heroic detective, the Saint. The squadron was disestablished in September 1945; the fictional character has outlived it by four decades, so far, and appeared on television as recently as last year. NAVAIR Archives

by the squadron. These aircraft were painted black, and were equipped with special radar and other electronic gear, represented on the emblem by the golden lightning bolts and radar . . . The outer red border represents the original red field of the squadron flag, from which the emblem was originally devised." By 1967, the insignia

The second version of VC-27's Saint added the elements of victory and the composite fighters and torpedo bombers. They adopted the character, according to the original submission to NAVAIR, because he represented "a force that strikes courageously and forcibly against its enemy, yet one that is too elusive to fall victim to the enemy's counter-force." NAVAIR Archives

Plate 7D.
VAQ-33, VAQ-33, VAQ-135, VAQ-132, VAQ-133, VAQ-136,
VAQ-131, VAQ-209, VAQ-138, VAQ-140, VAQ-141, VAQ-142

(plate 7B) showed a skull in center of a compass, directions around the outside, two sets of wings, and crossed torpedos.

VP–40 "Fighting Marlins"

In the mid 1950s, VP–40's design showed an angry marlin piercing a submarine, bubbles rising. Note the variations in the shape of the sub, the fish's back fin, and the bubbles in the two versions of this insignia that appear in plate 7B. The logo reappeared in the mid 1960s, but the sub is darker and at a slightly different angle, the bubble pattern is different and it has a banner that says "Laging Handa" at the top and "PATRON FORTY" at the bottom. VP–40 was established January 1951.

Plate 7E.
VAQ–129, VFC–12, VAQ–130, VAQ–134, VAQ–137, VAQ–138, VC–10, VAQ–139

This insignia preceded the celebrated "bat girl" now used by VP-24. The squadron was VP-HL-4, a heavy patrol squadron. Sharp-eyed aircraft spotters may detect the outline of a PB4Y-2 Privateer at upper left. NAVAIR Archives

Here she is—the only pinup left in the insignia archive. A potential girlfriend for Batman?

VP-44 "Golden Pelicans"

This squadron was established in January 1951. Along with the VP-40, it has survived four decades without a redesignation. See plate 7B. VP-44 currently flies out of NAS Brunswick, Maine.

VP-45 "Pelicans"

The insignia features a sedate pelican in front of a cloud, above a periscope (plate 7B). The squadron was established in 1942 as VP-205, and flew PBMs during World War II. The insignia dates from the 1940s.

The old VP-44 insignia adorns this pilot's flight jacket, circa 1971 at Atsugi, Japan. The two lieutenant commanders in the photo were filing a flight plan before taking off in their P-3 for a flight to the United States. USN

Plate 7F.
VRC–40, VFP–206, VAW–124, VC–1, VAW–127, VC–6, VAW–126,
VX–4, VX–5

VP-45's placid pelican hasn't changed since this February 1949 depiction. NAVAIR Archives

VP-48 "Boomerangers"

This insignia is a whole-bird version of the VS-27 design (plate 10E). The squadron was disestablished in 1950.

VP-52 "Black Cats"

Sometimes written VPB-52, for Patrol Bombing Squadron, VP-52 was another of the "Black Cat" squad-

rons of World War II. Insignia showed a winged elephant (upright) holding a telescope with its trunk and about to toss a round, black bomb, dated by one source back to 1929.

VS-21 "Fighting Redtails"

Plate 10E shows the insignia of an earlier VS-21, a genie on a magic carpet. This squadron was established in 1945 as CVEG-41. The current insignia, which dates from at least September 1956 (it appears in that issue of *Naval Aviation News*), is a broken sub against a shield emblazoned with lightning, with a moon at upper left and a knife at lower center (plate 7C).

VS-24 "Scouts"

The official insignia shows a bird of prey clutching a broken submarine (plate 7C). The unofficial one shows "The Duty Cat," a cartoon feline getting hit by lightning in the rear end (plate 7C). In 1960, when the current VS-24 was established, a *Naval Aviation News* article said, "The Duty Cat of VS-24 had taken up his old duties as guardian angel of squadron pilots and aircrewmen aboard USS *Valley Forge*. The last time he stood a watch was four years ago when the old squadron was disestablished. The Duty Cat took up his duties in 1948 when the original VS-24, composed of 18 torpedo bombers, reported for shake-down training aboard USS *Wright*, CVL-49. A young pilot/artist drew the lightning-struck feline on the ready room briefing board to indicate a squadron plane was still aloft. From that time on, it was decreed that flight operations would not begin until the ritual of placing the Cat on watch was accomplished. It became the duty of the junior flying officer to post the Cat . . . He grew from a chalk-drawn image . . . to a colored drawing on cardboard backing . . . to his present state of

VP-52's elephant with telescope in bomb once appeared in pink, surely one of the oddest insignia of all times. Naval Aviation News

VS-24's unofficial insignia, circa 1960. The Duty Cat is still a popular squadron insignia, and appeared on squadron T-shirts at Tailhook 1989 in Las Vegas. Naval Aviation News

Plate 7G.
VAW–78, RVAW–110, VAW–113, VAW–112, VAW–121, VAW–122,
VAW–123, VAW–125, VAW–120, VAW–120

fancy coloring on a plexiglas plaque. Somewhere along the way, he became the principal figure on the squadron insignia. Only those pilots and aircrewmen who had completed day and night carrier flight qualifications were permitted to wear the patch." One pilot applied for a patch, and the Navy found that he'd done some of his

Plate 7H.
VR-22, VR-58, VPB-151, VB-5, VT-31, VU-5, VFA-15,
VF(AW)-3, VT-2, VFA-87, VF(AW)-4, VT-1, VFA-136, VF-113

74

Plate 7I.
HS–5, HS–8, HS–8, HS–10, HS–15, HSL–32, HS–17, HSL–47,
HSL–35, HSL–40, HSL–34, HSL–43

Plate 7J.
HS-1, HS-3, HS-6, HS-7, HS-9, HS-4, HC-8, HS-11, HS-11,
HS-9, HS-16, HS-75

Plate 7K.
HC-2, HAL-4, HC-5, HM-18, HU-2, HC-7, HT-8, HC-1,
HM-12, HM-14, HC-4

night quals at twilight, not pitch darkness, so they gave him a patch with sunglasses on the cat.

"According to squadron legend, the article continued, "the original VS–24 operated without a shipboard fatality from the time the Duty Cat arrived until the squadron was decommissioned."

VS–31 "Topcats"

A recent squadron public affairs officer said that he didn't know the origin of this insignia (plate 7C), which shows a cat on a cloud, reaching for a swimming mouse (its tail is a periscope). "It apparently dates to the immediate post-war," he said. The squadron was established in

Plate 7L.
Carrier Air Wing 3, VF–161 aboard USS Midway, *Fighter Wing 1,*
Carrier Air Wing 13, Medium Attack Wing 1, Carrier Airborne Early
Warning Wing 12, Carrier Air Wing 30

1948; they were in the Suez in 1956, in Lebanon in 1958, in Berlin in 1962, and took part in astronaut recoveries during the *Mercury* and *Gemini* projects. VS–31 flies the S–3A out of NAS Cecil Field, Florida.

Chapter 8

Regulations and unofficial insignia

The military powers-that-be have always tried to keep a handle on the insignia dreamed up by those wild and crazy warriors out in the field. The inability of headquarters to fully control them, however, quickly became clear. "Insignia, by regulation, 'may be of caricature design, not necessarily classic or heraldic, but must be in good taste . . .'" wrote Gerard Hubbard in an article titled "Aircraft Insignia, Spirit of Youth" in the June 1943 issue of *National Geographic.* "The grinning, lively images are not permitted, technically, in zones of operation . . . [but] commanding officers have been known to wink at breaking the rule."

The astonishing popularity of the insignia was clear. "The squadron designs are so much in favor," Hubbard noted, "that without official approval so far . . . the aircraft insignia, in small size, generally embroidered, are worn as breast patches on the left pockets of flight jackets."

Another article in that issue dealt with Army Air Force insignia. It explained that "the underlying idea of such designs has the blessing of Gen. H. H. Arnold,

commander of all U.S. Army Air Forces." The AAF had approved 243 designs to date, and "others are coming in, through the AAF's own Insignia and Design Section, at the rate of two a day . . . For squadron insignia the proposals have a decidedly modern trend. But there are other designs, hundreds of them, which are staid and dignified. These are for headquarters squadrons . . ."

The Navy didn't lag behind in creating insignia, nor in issuing guidance for them. In May 1946, the Navy's official aviation magazine (*Naval Aviation News*) began running what would be a long-standing series of insignia inside its back cover. The caption says that squadrons should "submit their proposed insignia designs" in accordance with one of the articles in the BUAER manual, and that "Regulations that during the war prohibited the use of the color red in insignia and banned the incorporation of the actual designation are 'out.'" Since the illustrations are in black and white, however, it is hard to tell which squadrons took advantage of the change in rules.

Both the HU–1 and the VA–16A (plate 10F) designs, since they include the squadron designation, would not

These two versions of the same insignia show why Navy regulations quickly began to prohibit the use of designations (numbers, acronyms or *initializations) as part of the basic design—they changed too often.*
NAVAIR Archives

have been in accordance with the regulations for wartime designs. The purpose of printing the designation in the banner at the bottom was so that it could be removed during combat for security reasons.

In January 1950, *Naval Aviation News* returned to the topic of insignia in particular and aviation decorations in general. After the war, an article said, "coincident with the arrival of wives and families in areas once sacred to the fighting man, individual plane art fell into disrepute . . . Directives appeared banning promiscuous aircraft art." Whether promiscuous insignia were in use or were being proposed is unclear; nevertheless, magazine readers were given citations from an Aviation Circular Letter and a NAVAER Spec.: "Policy dictates that insignia shall not include number, designation or aircraft reproduction that may be replaced. Levity and bad taste are frowned upon. The insigne shall reflect dignity, originality and portray generally the mission of the unit."

The July 1948 design of VF–20–A is an example of the first prohibition—it shows the gold wings of naval aviation mounted on a sword that has flames around its tip. The design says "Fighting Squadron Twenty Able" around its outer rim. According to the policy, the slogan was not permissible.

Once again, you'll note, the Aviation Circular Letter mentioned sounds the dignity theme again. It would be a constant refrain in the decades to follow, and careful researchers will detect a note of frustration in the official pronouncements from Washington, D.C. The first real crackdown was launched in December 1952. "The days of Mickey Mouse and Alice the Goon on Navy squadron

Although this curious old insignia actually appeared in print in Naval Aviation News *magazine in February 1947, it is hard to imagine the powers-that-be giving it official approval. The upraised middle finger has had off-color implications since well before World War II.* NAVAIR Archives

insignia are numbered as the Navy moves to standardize and improve the caliber of its emblems," a *Naval Aviation News* article announced. "During World War II, squadrons came up with all manner of shoulder patches on their flight jackets and painted insignia on their planes. Some were pretty juvenile, many poorly drawn and obsolete . . ."

"In the old days, the sky was the limit on what could be included in insignia," the article continued. "Almost anything was approved but for lack of more definite 'ground rules,' the line outside the Chief of Naval Operations' door was filled with 'repeaters.' A squadron frequently had several different designs over a period of years." The solution, needless to say, was the issuance of an OPNAV Instruction, which promised to "bring some order out of the confusion [by] setting out some do's and don'ts."

The headquarters staff realized that some squadrons didn't have a member who could draw. For their benefit, and in an unusual and little-known instance of inter-service cooperation, the Navy enlisted "the aid of the Army's heraldic section to redraw some of the insignia so that something a little more appropriate and lasting would result."

Here are some of the rules mentioned in the 1952 article:
- "Heraldic portrayal of beasts, fowl, devices, instruments and weapons of the sea and air is preferred."
- "Place of commissioning, areas of operation, battle actions may be used, such as stars, terrain, flowers, trees."
- Designs should not include identifiable planes or ships, or unit or designation number."
- "Insigne should be designed so that it faces the observer's left and towards the enemy."
- "Morbid insignia should be avoided, those featuring skeletons, death's heads and the like."
- ". . . symbols denoting games of chance . . . are not suitable."

These rules would have wiped out the insignia of the "Grim Reapers," and the Marine's "Ace of Spades" squadron or the VF–82 design on plate 10A. The powerful popularity of existing insignia, however, was recognized. "Those squadron insignia already approved and in use will stay in effect until the squadron wants to change them," the article pointed out. "Then the new rules apply."

The 1952 recommendation that insignia include flowers must stand as one of the cheesiest, most unrealistic rules ever to trickle down the totem pole.

A footnote to the rules, added two years later, was that "Under CNO [Chief of Naval Operations] regulations, squadrons may be awarded the insigne of former famous squadrons not now active." VF–141 adopted the World War II insignia of the VF–14 "Iron Angels," for example.

Another iteration of insignia regulations appeared in 1974. It decreed that "the design should portray dignity rather than humor, although subtle humor presented in good taste is permissible. Ludicrous cartoons and gruesome portrayals are not acceptable."

Under these rules, the old VT-31 design, which showed Woody Woodpecker on a descending bomb with a slingshot, would not have been approved. The same goes for Felix and Oswald from the 1920s. Furthermore, under the "gruesome" clause, such designs as the Executioners from 1952, VC-5's grim reaper with a buzzard on his shoulder, and VS-22's submarine in a noose would have all been disapproved. The liquor bottle in the "Puckered Penguin's" left hand shows why another patch would never be officially approved (plate 8D).

Unofficial insignia

Multiplying the number of insignia that are floating around at any given time are a huge number of non-squadron insignia and patches. They include designs for detachments (called dets), air wings and air groups, ships,

---

"It's the new pansy Navy"

Squadron insignia are hidden from the general public. The Navy frowns on aviators wearing their flight jackets away from work, so most folks don't get to see the colorful patches. And since modern "tactical" paint schemes on aircraft have snuffed out all the bright reds and yellows, you'll see only a dark, silhouette-style version of the insignia on Navy aircraft at public air shows.

The current official paint job for Navy aircraft is called the Tactical Paint Scheme, or TPS. It specifies "an individual combination of three tones of gray" for each type of aircraft; squadron insignia are "a single TPS gray not to exceed 1,000 square inches in area." Each squadron can paint one aircraft—usually the skipper's—with a colorful tail.

That's a far cry from the old days. Back in the 1930s, there was an explosion of color, in part because of the rapid increase in number of squadrons, as well as the use of tail colors that were tied to aircraft carriers. In the early 1940s, color appeared on cowlings, bands around the aircraft's waist, propeller tips and rudders. The late 1950s and 1960s witnessed spectacular unit markings. Although the overall rule for carrier aircraft called for "light gull gray" on upper surfaces, with gloss white underneath, it still permitted what one writer called "extensive and colorful designs." This paint system lasted twenty years.

The sweeping changes are evident. Whereas in 1952, *Naval Aviation News* reported that "skeletons appear popular" among new designs. In 1968, the magazine reported that during the previous eighteen months, fifty-two had been approved, and that "all are in keeping with the dignity of the service." No skulls appeared.

Marilyn Hewitt, a civilian illustrator who works for the Navy and who draws insignia for Atlantic Fleet ships, is more blunt. "It's the new pansy Navy, that's what I call it. You can go out and kill," she observes, "but you can't imply that in your insignia."

Navy captain Zip Rausa recently retired as director of Naval Aviation History, and was on the board that ruled on proposed designs. Some of the rules are logical, he said. "You can't depict an actual airplane, only a generic one, because when a squadron changes aircraft, it might be a problem."

"Anything cartoon is kind of frowned upon," he continued. "You can't depict an animal performing a human-like task." Asked why, he replied, "I don't know. I don't think the SPCA got involved, however." As a result of this rule, designs such as the jaunty frog of VT-19, which is giving the thumbs-up sign, would be disapproved. It was approved in 1976, however.

In a typical month, Rausa said, they would get five requests, of which maybe one would be rejected. "The first one that shocked us in a while came from a volunteer training unit, in the reserves." Members of these units drill for points toward retirement only—they don't get paid. Their design had a dollar sign with a slash mark through it. "Technically we had no objection, but we thought it was in poor taste," Rausa said. They would also get calls from squadrons that had already ordered patches but wanted approval. In some cases, Rausa said he would counsel them to just use the insignia unofficially; in other words, they couldn't use it as a tail marking for an aircraft.

There were about 275 approved designs in 1986. Even though some of the classic designs don't conform to official guidance, Rausa said, "We think they're terrific for heritage purposes." One existing insignia seems custom-made to stir up the feminist element in Washington: the bat girl used by Patrol Squadron 24, the "Batmen," whose insignia is the only officially approved one depicting a pinup girl. However, Rausa said, "To my knowledge, there's never been a big flap about it."

An outstanding entry in the sub-genre of insignia that include skulls, this one was used by VF-133. Official prohibition of "gruesome" displays has eliminated most of the skulls, with a few notable exceptions. The blood dripping from this skull's teeth certainly qualifies as gruesome. NAVAIR Archives

This aviator gives the place of honor not to his squadron patch but to the patch from Air Wing 11, symbolized by two dice that add up to that number. Air Wing 11 deployed aboard USS Kitty Hawk (CVA–63).
Naval Aviation News

Another unofficial patch from the Vietnam era.

naval air stations, designs that commemorate an event or a cruise, and patches that mark an achievement (such as a hundred traps or a missile shoot, shown in plate 7N).

The F–14 has generated its own patch industry. The now-classic Tomcat cartoon character (plate 9A) has spun off dozens, perhaps hundreds of variations including those from F–14 squadrons, specialties (such as TARPS) and even foreign countries.

Often the intent was humorous, and many unofficial designs incorporated cartoons. An Al Capp creation, called a Kigmy, was adopted by Marine Fighter Squadron 122 in 1950. "The familiar Kigmy has donned a jet pilot's crash helmet and will appear on membership cards to be issued to VMF–122 pilots, who have completed the seat-ejection indoctrination course," the squadron announced.

Why that particular character, which gets kicked around in the comic strip? "Marine pilots going through the seat-ejection school and Kigmies have plenty in common," one Marine captain said. "Nothing to really kick about, you understand, but we do get booted."

Dozens of other unofficial insignia have been worn on flight jackets throughout the fleet. One belonged to VF–32, which was once nicknamed the "White Lightning" squadron, because they had a red-edged white lightning bolt on the nose of their aircraft. Their unofficial logo showed a hillbilly shooting a long rifle and riding on a jet-propelled jug of moonshine.

VA–52's regular insignia shows a knight wielding a mace and riding a turtle. During one cruise, the pilots got mad at having to fly so many tanker hops (delivering fuel to airborne planes), so they had a patch made up that

This tail marking is unusual for several reasons, one being that it shows an unofficial insignia. Almost every squadron that flies F–14s seems to have come up with some version featuring the Tomcat character.

showed a gas pump in the background and the knight holding the pump nozzle instead of a mace. The squadron skipper was not amused; he banished the patch from the flight jackets.

VF–84's hobo (plate 10K) is another classic unofficial design, with a red nose (from drinking, no doubt), a cigar, a hole in the shoe and "orders" in hand.

Sometimes the humor in an unofficial patch is clearly for insiders. For example, AOMs ("All Officers Meetings") in squadrons are known for being excruciatingly dull, thus the yawning mouth of the "O" (plate 8A). Crew members aboard USS *Midway* (CV–41) were exasperated when Ronald Reagan referred to them as "the other carrier" in a news conference in which the President remembered the names of the two aircraft carriers that arrived later (plate 8D).

At other times, the humor is unintentional. When crew members aboard USS *Midway* wanted to commemorate their record-breaking time on station during a deployment, the first version came back (from their Japanese contractor) with the numbers reversed (plate 8A).

After the August 1986 to March 1987 Mediterranean cruise, some of the JOs (junior officers) from VF–32 had an unofficial patch made up (plate 8D). It shows the wake of the carrier in the shape of a question mark, superimposed over a map of the Mediterranean Sea, with the slogans "Why manage when you can over-react" and "JFK 'Stop Making Sense' Med Cruise '86–'87" at the top and bottom. The idea, says former squadron member Lt. Ward Carroll, came from a TARPS (Tactical Air Reconnaisance Photography) photo of the ship in which the wake actually formed a question mark. It expressed well the feelings of the aircrews about the cruise: nothing really happened. They ran out of money for flight time, and there was a general feeling of pointlessness. They mail-ordered 300 of the patches and sold them for $5 a shot.

Non-squadron insignia come from a plethora of aviation-related sources, and appear as decals, patches or

Off-color slogans are not unknown on unofficial patches. This one, worn by A-6 pilot Lt. Cdr. Andy Keith, dates from his tour with VA-34 in 1977. The patch commemorates a frantic week of operations aboard USS John F. Kennedy *when the ship's fueling systems were down, so that all the tankers had to launch in the morning, fuel up on the beach, then return to refuel the other aircraft airborne over the boat. Keith recalls that they passed a million pounds of fuel in five days. FART stands for Fleet Air Refueling Team.*

Ordinary traps are exciting enough, but night traps are the ne plus ultra *of tailhook aviation, adrenalin-producing enough to merit their own mark of recognition. When you get 100 traps, you qualify as a "centurion"—TACAIR (tactical air, namely fighter and attack) guys all make it eventually, but tallying 100 on your first cruise is quite an accomplishment. Usually one of the senior officers in the squadron hands out the patch at an informal squadron ceremony.*

Plate 8A.
USS Midway; *an air-group composed of the insignia of VF–41,*
VF–21, VA–86, and VA–42; Carrier Air Group 11 (dice on star); USS

Coral Sea; *USS* Midway; *USS* Bennington *(CVA–20); AOM patch*
worn by attack pilot during the '70s.

84

Plate 8B.
Task force patch from an 1988 deployment; VA–87 commemorative;
Vietnam-era fighter pilot commemorative; Task Force 78; USS Prince-
ton; Torpedo-Bomber Squadron 29; USS Independence, 1981;
nameplate from an Air Force aggressor squadron based at Nellis AFB,
Nevada; Navy Fighter Weapons School, NAS Miramar, Calif.

both. "Topscope" (plate 8B) used to be a ground school for NFOs, which was part of "Topgun." Cruise and action commemoratives (plate 8B) come in all sizes—Vietnam-era "medals" (plate 8B shows one that contains an obscene phrase garbed in mock-Vietnamese, aimed at Uncle Ho). Air-wing and air-group decals (plate 7L) deco-

rate a lot of clipboards in the fleet; occasionally you'll see a patch version of one on a flight jacket, but not often.

Although USS *Bunker Hill* and USS *Wasp* (plate 10B) have squadron-like designs, the others reveal a combination of blandness and clutter that is typical of non-squadron insignia.

Plate 8C.
Patches are from the collection of Cdr. John "Pogo" Reid, an F–14 RIO: The "Mickey Knaus Club" was named after the squadron skipper during a VF–101 deployment aboard USS America *in 1971, flying F–4Js; the VF–101 Det O meant "Detachment Oceana," since the main squadron was still in Key West, pre 1970; a Mediterranean cruise*

commemorative from the early '70s, and a humorous takeoff on the Tonkin Gulf patch; Philippine hot spot and must-see for liberty hounds; USS America *double-centurion patch, circa 1972; Vietnam commemorative; VF–171, which was the F–4 RAG and was disestablished in the early '80s when the Navy ceased all F–4 training.*

Plate 8D.
F–14 aircrew commemorative, circa late 1970s; VF–41; VA–115; Air Development Squadron 6; VA–95, 1977; VA–72 Vietnam cruise commemorative, '66–'67; Mediterranean cruise commemorative, '82; USS John F. Kennedy, 1986–87; Iranian crisis, circa 1979; USS Midway (CV–41); Khaddafi calling card.

Plate 8E.
From the author's personal collection. A "Hey Joe" is a native vendor who sells stuff from a cart at the pier in liberty ports; the author picked up the nickname after very successfully marketing t-shirts and posters on his ship and at his squadron's home base.

Chapter 9

Trends in insignia

Although the Navy bureaucracy has repeatedly tried to get a handle on patches by specifying their content and design, the preferences and habits of individual squadrons and pilots have varied widely. For every trend in patches, there is almost always a counter-trend. In some squadrons, aviators wear the same patch in the same place, Air Force style; in other units, it is a free-for-all. Some pilots wear four, six, even ten patches on a jacket; others don't wear any. Some put patches on their leather jacket and leave their Nomex jacket plain; others reverse this habit. Some squadrons stick with old, tried-and-true designs for decades; others discard their current insignia and design a new one every few years.

Nevertheless, since the early 1940s, a number of minor and major trends have appeared (and usually disappeared). Recognizing them helps make sense of the sometimes bewildering and contradictory elements that play into the pageant of squadron insignia.

It is extremely difficult to categorize the kinds of things that have been included in the designs of squadron insignia. During the early years, and especially during World War II, a belligerent, motorcycle-gang philosophy was prevalent. Images of violence—clubs, bombs, skeletons, boxing gloves, fangs and such—were common and popular. For example, the insignia of the Army's 25th Bombardment Squadron, adopted in 1917, showed an executioner; notches in his axe stood for bombing mis-

Owners of G–1s have developed a spectrum of patch-wearing habits: some wear only one or two, others wear up to a dozen. Some wear patches only on their leather jacket, or only on their nylon jacket. This Navy commander, a fighter RIO, wears patches from five squadrons and several cruises (200 traps on USS John F. Kennedy, 200 on USS Midway and 300 on USS Ike).

A sampler of unofficial patches: a couple of centurion patches (signifying 100 carrier landings) appear on the back of the jacket worn by the man at the right, as well as a (CAG–11 WESTPAC—Western Pacific Carrier Air Group 11) cruise patch from 1984, and a "Top Eleven Tailhook" memento for a record number of traps.

sions credited to each pilot. A modern insignia, used by VS-25 (plate 10E), shows a mailed fist squeezing blood out of a submarine.

At the same time, there were elements of off-beat humor, idiosyncratic designs and things of a purely local significance. There were well-known cartoons (Jiggs, Barney Google or Felix), with a small subset of what we now call editorial cartoons—a booted foot kicking the Kaiser, for example, during World War I. Other designs were based on puns or popular slang of the day—the "Hat in the Ring," for example.

Some insignia had elaborate, complex derivations (see the explanation of VP-12's insignia in chapter 4). Others were so off-handed as to seem snide; the Tophatters is the classic example of that. Sometimes elements of the designs were quite straightforward. When Navy fighter squadrons flew Panthers, for example, images of that animal populated the insignia. VF-781 had a panther surrounded by flames, nose at low left, against a star in a circle. VF-51 had a crouching panther. Of the famous "Black Cat" squadrons that flew Catalinas, VP-44, VP-33, VP-12 and VP-71 all had felines in their insignia.

Slogans on patches (plate 10N) seem to have been quite popular during the Korean era.

In all cases, the squadron members drew up designs for themselves, not for the public or for publicity purposes. This fact adds a great deal of both mystery and richness to the study of insignia.

An identifiable trend, going back to the very birth of military insignia, is the polarity of graphic energy—what we might call the "saltiness factor"—among the various designs. In the old days, the front-line combat squadrons tended to have vivid, explicit designs, while the headquarters squadrons had dull, mechanical designs. In the Navy, aircraft carrier insignia seem to have a snoozy, corny, chamber-of-commerce flavor, a trend that has continued under the current regulations. The ongoing battle between the staid and dignified and the morbid is detailed in chapter 8.

This debate isn't restricted to the Navy headquarters and squadron artists, however. It spilled over into the pages of a magazine called *Wings of Gold* (the magazine of the Association of Naval Aviation) in 1988, producing a wonderful series of letters to the editor.

That winter, *Wings of Gold* ran a cover photo of a handsome young pilot wearing a flight jacket with the squadron patch of Fighter Squadron 143 on the breast. The patch itself shows an innocuous silhouette of a griffin, and the attached logo bears the squadron's nickname: the "Pukin' Dogs." It is a somewhat sophomoric (and therefore extremely popular) logo.

One reader promptly wrote in to complain about the gross nickname. "During my time in the service," he wrote, "we did some controversial things but none of them were in such poor taste . . . It is beyond me how any C.O. could approve such a patch or be proud to lead a group that would want to wear it."

This letter stirred up a storm of defensive rebuttals, and the next issue of the magazine brought on the

defense. One reader (a retired squadron commanding officer) said he was disgusted with the complaint. "Remember," he chided, "combat aviation is not child's play based on idealistic, moral values issued by wimpy non-participants." Another reader figured the complaint must have been tongue-in-cheek: "Behind each set of Navy Wings is a man who is a warrior par excellence and at the same time there is a boy full of hell and rarin' to go," he wrote. "The mischievous boys are always at work. Satire, sarcasm and cynicism offset the tedium of life at sea and the sometimes rather self-righteous character our seniors bestow on themselves."

Rear Adm. Chuck McGrail, a former "Pukin' Dog," wrote, "I took as much pride in that title as in being an Iron Angel, Silverking, Fighting Falcon or Peacemaker. I don't think any of us felt his maturity or taste at question due to the squadron nickname—other things perhaps, but not that label . . . I don't know of a Pukin' Dog who isn't proud of the name—probably because they all had a good sense of proportion and a fine sense of humor . . . in our business, you need both."

That statement, you'd hope, would settle the argument once and for all. History, unfortunately, indicates otherwise.

The tremendous number of squadrons, the similarity between them, and the resulting explosion of insignia have produced another problem—repetition. Among nicknames, some is probably unavoidable. To the term Fighting, for instance, you can now add Aardvarks, Renegades, Checkmates or Saints.

Naval Aviation News *had already published hundreds of photos of Navy and Marine aviators wearing leather flight jackets when the first patch appeared on one of those jackets in this photo from the Oct. 15, 1945 issue.* Naval Aviation News

89

Plate 9A
The now-classic Tomcat design (top center) has spun off dozens, perhaps hundreds of variations including F-14 squadrons (such as VF-14, third row, right), specialties (such as TARPS, bottom center) and even foreign countries (Iranian version in right column, second from top).

Navy Lt. Mark Morgan discussed another aspect of the problem of repetition when he wrote a letter to *The Hook,* published in the summer issue of 1987. He wrote that the establishing of new squadrons offers the "rare opportunity to resurrect some of the more historic and memorable squadrons and emblems . . . yet someone somewhere has apparently missed the point." Morgan pointed out that there are ten different squadrons with the name hawk in them. "We're seeing a run on smallish fighting birds," he observed. "When compared to some of the classic insignia (as depicted in *The Hook*), we're seeing a lot of unimaginative emblems." He also decried the trend

of redoing insignia whenever a squadron transitions to a new aircraft. "VF–111 went through this drill for years," Morgan wrote, but "somewhere along the line, cooler heads remembered that the Sundowners achieved their name and fame in WWII, and that F4Fs on the insignia were appropriate and timeless."

Usually, older insignia are discarded in favor of newer designs. Sometimes the reverse is true. One squadron traded a newer design for an old one from the early 1950s, which showed a hunting falcon perched on a mailed fist. A squadron member found it while rooting around in the squadron archives. The motto on the design was the word "Dirigimus," which means "we direct"; the squadron's task is to control aircraft during amphibious assaults.

The manner in which aviators wear patches has also been through lots of fads since the 1940s. Once again, the pages of *Naval Aviation News* document the changing habits.

A May 1950 photo of VF–43 shows the squadron members posed on the deck of USS *Midway.* All wear G–1s, but of the thirteen men in the photo, only four have patches on the breast, and only two of those are similar (the large green pawn used at various times by VF–42 and VA–42).

The first of what would become traditional—most members of a squadron wearing the same patch in the same place—doesn't appear in a photo until June 1951, when members of VF–11, the "Red Rippers," posed on the flight deck of USS *Coral Sea* with two former skippers who had since made admiral. Almost all members have a large Ripper patch on the right breast. Two have it on the left breast, with a different patch on the right. One man wears the Ripper patch on his upper left sleeve, and another wears it on his upper right sleeve.

Photos from the early and mid 1950s show lots of G–1s with one or two patches on them. One of the earliest multi-patch jackets appears in a September 1953 photo, worn by a lieutenant whose squadron was flying off USS *Boxer* and who has at least four patches on his G–1. A July 1959 photo of a Navy commander (who was the first Navy pilot to check out in a SAC B–52) shows patches above and below his nametag on the left front of his jacket, a patch on his left sleeve and another patch on the right breast.

A final trend of note—in general, patches have gotten much smaller through the years. In 1955, according to photos from that period, some sleeve patches were huge, as much as six or eight inches long. One 1965 photo shows an aviator with a patch that is about twelve inches around, sewn on the back of his G–1. The current rules specify a four-inch disk, to which scrolls may be added above and below. In practice, there is ample deviation, in shape and size, although the largest patches rarely exceed five inches.

Chapter 10

Collections and collectors

Patches cry out for collecting: they are colorful, distinctive, available and they range from cheap to horrendously valuable. They are easy to store and display, as well. For these reasons, collecting patches is a booming field, knit together by the American Society of Military Insignia Collectors, or ASMIC. ASMIC breaks down the sub-specialties of collecting into ten categories: distinctives, patches, medals, ribbons, cap badges, rank badges, foreign, insignia of the world, unit histories and wings. The Society has thousands of members from around the world, publishes a newsletter and a magazine, sponsors annual national and regional shows, and skillfully keeps its members in touch with each other.

A true collector is the sort of person who would instantly recognize that the USS *Princeton* patch (plates 8B and 10C) is partially embroidered canvas, as opposed to fully embroidered.

Member Dennis Covello of New Jersey said that the "general militaria collectors" call patch collectors "rag pickers," but it doesn't seem to bother him. He started collecting in 1961, concentrating on Army patches, but has expanded his focus over the years. He branched into Navy and Marine Corps items around 1970, accumulating a large collection of Navy shoulder tabs, and now reports that he has a patch from more than ninety-five percent of every active Navy and Marine Corps unit (including reserves).

Covello mounts his patches on 5x8 inch cards, then stashes them in small boxes. He files them by squadron type and squadron number. If he displayed all of his

Plate 10A.
From The Hook, *Spring, 1984*

Plate 10B.
From The Hook, *Summer, 1984*

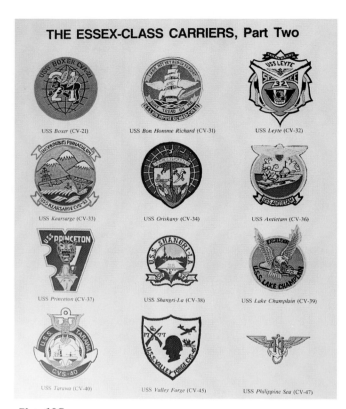

THE ESSEX-CLASS CARRIERS, Part Two

USS *Boxer* (CV-21)

USS *Bon Homme Richard* (CV-31)

USS *Leyte* (CV-32)

USS *Kearsarge* (CV-33)

USS *Oriskany* (CV-34)

USS *Antietam* (CV-36)

USS *Princeton* (CV-37)

USS *Shangri-La* (CV-38)

USS *Lake Champlain* (CV-39)

USS *Tarawa* (CV-40)

USS *Valley Forge* (CV-45)

USS *Philippine Sea* (CV-47)

Plate 10C.
From The Hook, *Winter, 1984*

patches, he said, "I could fill every square inch of the ceilings and walls on my house, all three floors."

Another ASMIC member, Lyndon Meredith of Virginia Beach, Virginia, was introduced to patch collecting by his mother, who once worked at a military base in Washington state. She gave him a cigar box full of patches that she'd accumulated, and he in turn started tracking down the history of some of the units. He has been collecting for thirty years. Many of his prized patches, he pointed out, "I got back when they were fifty cents or a dollar." Even so, he said, "I wish I'd started when I was 5 or 6 years old, right after the war."

Although he modestly claims that there are plenty of patch collectors with larger and more elaborate collections, Meredith's hoard is certainly respectable. He recently estimated his collection at somewhere between 10,000 and 15,000 patches. He generously allowed many of his patches to be photographed for this book, but points out that Navy stuff is only a sideline. Most of his Navy patches date from World War II to the mid 1950s. His main collecting fields are World War I and World War II Army, and submarines.

Meredith's most recent project is a 4x6 foot display board of all Air Force (and AAF) shoulder sleeve insignia, showing World War II to current. It took him about a year to finish.

He has seen patch prices rise steadily through the years. Back in the 1970s, he had a collection stolen that he

CARRIER-BASED HS SQUADRONS 1952-1985

HS-1

HELASRON TWO

TRIDENTS HS-3

HS-4 BLACK KNIGHTS

HELANTISUBRON FIVE

HELANTISUBRON SIX

HS-7

HELANTISUBRON EIGHT

HS-9 SEA GRIFFINS

HELANTISUBRON TEN

HS-11

HELANTISUBRON TWELVE

HS-13 SUB CHOPPERS

HELANTISUBRON 14

HELANTISUBRON FIFTEEN

HELANTISUBRON SEVENTEEN

Plate 10D.
From The Hook, *Fall, 1985*

THE ORIGINAL VS SQUADRONS 1945-1955

VS-20

VS-21

VS-23

VS-22

VS-25

VS-27

VS-26

VS-36

VS-37

VS-32

VAIRASRON 38

Plate 10E.
From The Hook, *Fall, 1985*

figures was worth about $20,000. "Certain patches I had back then I'll never recover," he said. He still has some patches that dealers would charge $400 to $600 for. Adding rare ones is increasingly difficult, of course. "My wife bought me *one* patch for Christmas last year," he said. "It was from a squadron that was around in the late '40s and early '50s. It cost $275."

He has also acquired hundreds of reference books, recently adding a useful one about Vietnam and a couple that deal with AAF bomber squadrons. He says that in general the Navy tends to be the weakest service when it comes to documentation.

A collector named Steve Ginsberg was featured in *Naval Aviation News* in 1974. Ginsberg was then twenty-seven, and had just spent part of his honeymoon in Washington, D.C. at the Naval Aviation history office, tracking down information about insignia. Ginsberg's collection then included 600 patches. "Over the years he has tenaciously issued a fusillade of letters to just about every aviation command in the Navy," the article said. "His barrage of question-saturated requests to the aviation history office reached impossible proportions." Ginsberg figured he'd written about 2,500 letters to squadrons and commands asking for patches. In one case, he wrote twelve letters over a seven-year span until he got a patch. Three years later, he was back in the magazine, checking in with 1,048 patches.

The official Navy has tried to get into the collecting business through the years, with unknown success. One

Plate 10G.
From The Hook, *Fall, 1987*

Plate 10F.
From The Hook, *Spring, 1986*

Plate 10H.
From The Hook, *Spring. 1988*

Plate 10I.
From The Hook, *Winter, 1988*

of the most ambitious plans for a display was announced in the December 1959 issue of *Naval Aviation News,* which issued a call from the Deputy Chief of Naval Operations (Air) for "a display of their approved insignia on the bulkheads of the OpNav passageways in the Pentagon. Each squadron, group, station or activity is being asked to provide a reproduction of its insigne in color." Whether the display materialized, and how long it lasted, is unknown.

In July 1971, however, another call from the same source appeared in the magazine. The goal was again a display of the insignia of "all aviation commands of the Navy," to be mounted on "the bulkheads of the OpNav passageways in the Pentagon." The success of this later campaign is also unknown.

Readers of *The Hook,* the magazine published by the Tailhook Association, know that editor Bob Lawson has accumulated a tremendous collection of patches, particularly unofficial ones. The magazine has a regular feature called "Insigniamania," which is a gold mine of information about origins and derivations of Navy insignia. The inside back cover of the magazine has also run excellent color renditions of old patches. A number of the plates in this book are reprinted from those covers.

Another collection of insignia (in the form of decals rather than patches) is at the Naval Aviation Depot (NAD) in Norfolk, Virginia. The decal shop there is one of the hidden and probably vanishing places that played a role in the development and history of Navy insignia. Buried

Plate 10J.
From The Hook, *Spring, 1989*

Plate 10K.
From The Hook, *Summer, 1986*

deep in the dim catacombs of a converted World War II hangar, the decal shop's walls sport a wonderful collection of rare and obscure insignia. Graphics art mechanic John Parker, who first came to work at the NAD in 1949, remembers many of the origins.

On the walls are a cheshire cat, tigers and eagles in every conceivable position, Albert the Alligator from "Pogo" wielding a machine gun, and a cat getting hit in the rear by a lightning bolt. High on one wall is a large decal of the famous (or infamous) cartoon African native; the insignia banner says "PATRON FIVE, The Savage Sons." Parker refers to it as a Ubangi, and dates it from the 1950s. The provenance of this design is muddled—VA–12, which dates from May 1945, is now called the "Flying Ubangis." In the summer of 1979 at NAS Cecil Field, Florida, they called themselves the "World Famous Flying Ubangis." The current VP–5 goes back to 1937.

Parker recalls doing a Felix that was carrying a lobster in the mid 1970s, because VF–31 was making so many lobster runs up to NAS Brunswick, Maine. "They took a lot of ribbing about that," he said. The insignia reads "LOB-RON 31," and bears an overscript that says, "We get ours at night." He remembers when VAW–122 changed their design from an eagle to a plain, cartoon shark with the motto "Steeljaw," which was their old call sign.

According to Parker, the staff at the decal shop used to make thousands of little half-inch round decals that people could put on cigarette lighters. They have also

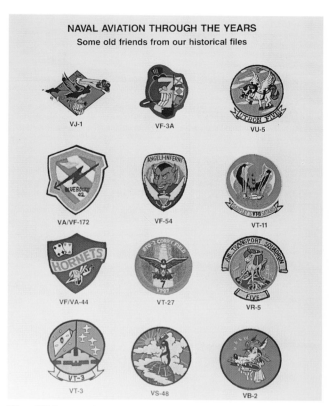

Plate 10M.
From The Hook, *Spring, 1987*

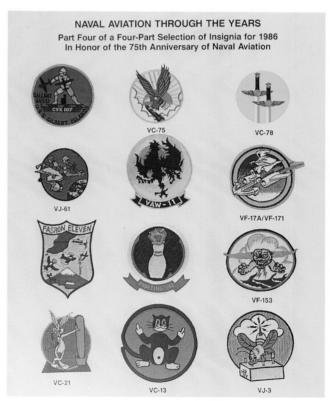

Plate 10L.
From The Hook, *Winter, 1986*

Plate 10N.
From The Hook, *Summer, 1989*

THE AJ AND A3D
HEAVY ATTACK SQUADRONS
Focusing on Early VC/VAH
Squadron Insignia

Plate 100.
From The Hook, *Winter, 1989*

made decals as large as five feet wide for the tail of a P–3. Of the smaller sizes, he explained, "Bases use them to play tricks on each other. We did some of a tiger with an ice bag on his head, so it looked like he was sick." Known as "zappers," the stickers show up everywhere once a squadron hits town. Parker recalls seeing one on the ceiling of a house of ill repute in Las Vegas.

In general, Parker isn't a fan of the current insignia regulations. "The new ones are a lot plainer than the old ones," he said. "They're getting a little milder." He misses the cartoons.